William K. Klingaman

TURNING 40

Wit, Wisdom & Whining

A PLUME BOOK

PLUME
Published by the Penguin Group
Penguin Books USA Inc., 375 Hudson Street,
New York, New York 10014, U.S.A.
Penguin Books Ltd, 27 Wrights Lane, London W8 5TZ, England
Penguin Books Australia Ltd, Ringwood, Victoria, Australia
Penguin Books Canada Ltd, 10 Alcorn Avenue,
Toronto, Ontario, Canada M4V 3B2
Penguin Books (N.Z.) Ltd, 182–190 Wairau Road,
Auckland 10, New Zealand

Penguin Books Ltd, Registered Offices:
Harmondsworth, Middlesex, England

First published by Plume, an imprint of New American Library,
a division of Penguin Books USA Inc.

First published by Plume, an imprint of Dutton Signet,
a division of Penguin Books USA Inc.

First Printing, July, 1992
20 19 18 17 16 15 14 13

℗ REGISTERED TRADEMARK—MARCA REGISTRADA

LIBRARY OF CONGRESS CATALOGING-IN-PUBLICATION DATA
Turning 40 : wit, wisdom, and whining / [compiled by] William K.
   Klingaman.
        p.   cm.
     ISBN 0-452-26821-4
     1. Middle age—Humor.   2. Middle age—Quotations, maxims, etc.
   3. Middle age—Psychological aspects.   I. Klingaman, William A.
   II. Title: Turning forty.
   PN6231.M47T87   1992
   305.24′4—dc20
                                                          91-42617
                                                            CIP
Printed in the United States of America
Set in Palatino
Designed by Eve L. Kirch

For my brother, who is two years older than I.

ACKNOWLEDGMENTS

This has been one of the most enjoyable books I have ever written, and so I would like to thank my agent, Don Cutler, for persuading me to take on this project. Thanks also to my editor, Matt Sartwell, and all the good people at New American Library for coming up with the concept in the first place.

I would like to express my gratitude to Nolan Ryan and Jerry Greenfield for agreeing to share their thoughts on turning 40; it would be a better world if everyone would maintain their youthful outlook. Thanks to Renee Hershey for helping me locate 40th birthday cards, and to Hallmark Cards for graciously permitting me to reprint them; to Sally Barrett and Dr. Susan Blumenthal of the National Institute of Mental Health; to Dan Rodricks of the Baltimore *Sun*; and to Jeff Jones of Nielsen Media Research.

More than anyone else, however, my wife, Janet, deserves my appreciation. Like me, she recently turned 40, and had no problems with it at all until I started working on this book. Now we can both look forward to turning 41.

CONTENTS

No wise man ever wished to be younger.
—JONATHAN SWIFT

Age doesn't matter, unless you're a cheese.
—JOHN PAUL GETTY

A VIEW FROM

If you are now 40 years old and feeling rather sore about it, or if you are closing in on 40 and are beginning to worry a bit about the whole procedure (no, it doesn't hurt, unless your eyes are going bad and you stub your toe on the cat), or if you turned 40 a while back and just want to remember how it felt to trip over the edge, this book is for you. It is also for those millions of men and women who crossed the same boundary centuries ago and, unfortunately, will never be able to purchase a copy.

Forty has long been considered a special milestone in life. In ancient China, at the time of Confucius, positions of political power were reserved for men who were 40 or older, on the assumption that maturity and judgment arrived at that age. The number 40 turns up repeatedly in Eastern civilization at critical points in the lives of philosophers and spiritual leaders. For instance, the Chinese sage Mencius was 40 when he attained wisdom, and, according to legend, the Buddha's mother was 40 years old when the Enlightened One himself was born—which, incidentally, gives her something in common with Danny De Vito's mother.

For the Jewish people, too, the number 40 was filled with symbolic significance. Moses was 40 years old when he first came to realize his kinship with the Jews in Egypt; he was twice 40 when he led his people out of the Pharoah's grasp, and was three times 40 when the wandering tribes reached the Promised Land. The greatest kings of Israel, David and Solomon, both reigned for 40 years. And Hillel, the most famous Pharisee in the history of Judaism, was 40 when he came to Jerusalem to begin studying with the masters. The same tradition carried over into Arabic culture; according to the Koran, the prophet Mohammad was 40 when he first received the divine revelations that gave birth to the Muslim faith.

Roman historians believed that most people accomplished little of note before they were 40; in fact, if Roman scholars did not know a ruler's birthdate, they established it by simply counting back 40 years from his first major triumph. On the other hand, a large percentage of the Roman population never made it to 40 at all, and for those who did, Cicero informs us that old age was thought to begin at the age of 46.

Still, this was definitely an advance over primitive man—and woman—who were considered essentially obsolete at 40, with their peak productive and reproductive years behind them. And for centuries after the fall of Rome, only the favored few in European society reached the age of 40. Peasants who made it as far as 30 were considered lucky, wrinkled, and very old. In *The Inferno*, Dante declared 35 to be the prime of life; after that, it was all downhill to hell and gone. As late as the seventeenth century, the average life span in France—a reasonably civilized country, by contemporary standards—was from 20 to 25 years; most adults died between 30 and 40.

Conditions were only slightly better in America, especially on the frontier. As Robert Benchley explained in his landmark study on the subject, "Life Begins at (fill in the space)," "In the old days there was perhaps some reason for growing old after 40, or possibly for not even reaching 40 at all. The Indians did a great deal toward making a man feel unfit at an early age. If you had to spend the day hewing through great trees and great bowls of corn-meal mush with a coon-skin cap on, and then found yourself in the evening having to look around all over the house for your scalp, there might be some excuse for your saying: 'I'm all in, Bessie! I guess I must be getting old.' "

Obviously, the notion of turning 40 still carried drastic implications in the United States at the beginning of this century, when the average life expectancy for women in America was 51 (and only 48 for men), and middle age thus began somewhere in the neighborhood of 30. Compare that to the current average life spans of more than 70 years, and the expectation that we will be living even longer—by 2020, 40 will be the median age of the American population.

So relax and enjoy a sense of camaraderie with those who, like the people in this book, have gone before you across the threshold, because now is a great time to turn 40. If you choose to attempt to stem the ravages of time, your options have never been more numerous: moisturizing creams and Retin-A to smooth the wrinkles, exercise videos to flatten your stomach and tone your thighs, and a host of cosmetic surgeons from uptown Manhattan to Beverly Hills. And if you are one of those countless millions (bless them) who prefer to let nature take its course (mostly downward and outward), rest assured that our culture no longer considers 40 to be old or over the hill. Now it's 50 you have to watch out for.

Have fun with the quotes and lists that follow. If the humor seems a little dark at times, keep looking for the light at the end of the tunnel—it's always there. Personally, I turned 40 several years ago, and was doing fine until

Reprinted with permission from Hallmark Cards, Inc.

my opthalmologist, who could not possibly be a day over 30, told me I needed trifocals, and launched into a lengthy discussion of what happens to your eyesight after you pass your 40th birthday. So the next time I see the little whippersnapper (and now I *can* see him), I will have all these wonderful things to tell him about turning 40 . . . except that I'll probably have forgotten them all by then.

ON BEING

There is much to be said for—and against—turning 40, and here are a few particularly noteworthy opinions on the matter, ranging all the way from cheerful acceptance through stoic resignation to outright hostility. My own favorite selection comes from British comedian and erstwhile Monty Python member John Cleese: "Once you get into your forties, I think you start to let go of any last lingering notion that life makes any sense, or that society can ever be organized really satisfactorily. Let go of that, and almost everything seems to be funny."

Even politicians, prime-time network television, and rap music.

◆ ◆ ◆ ◆

"Forty is the old age of youth."　　　　　　—VICTOR HUGO

"Too old to rock 'n' roll, too young to die."

—JETHRO TULL

"After all, it isn't a crime to be forty. A pity maybe, but not a crime." —JACK BENNY

"Look at me, now that I am 40 years old. So what?" —BRIGITTE BARDOT

"This is what forty looks like. We've been lying about it so long, who would know?" —GLORIA STEINEM

"Forty is the real Awkward Age; you are old enough to realize that you would look silly doing things you are still young enough to wish you could do." —ROBERT M. YODER

"It seems that only yesterday I was fifteen and old people were people of forty, who were always going someplace to sit down." —BILL COSBY

"At fifteen I thought only of study; at thirty I began playing my role; at forty I was sure of myself." —CONFUCIUS

"At twenty years of age, the will reigns; at thirty, the wit; at forty, the judgment." —BENJAMIN FRANKLIN

"When you are forty, half of you belongs to the past." —JEAN ANOUILH

"A man of forty is a fool to wonder at any thing." —DANIEL WEBSTER

"Any man of forty who is endowed with moderate intelligence has seen—in the light of the uniformity of nature—the entire past and future." —MARCUS AURELIUS

"Be wise with speed; a fool of forty is a fool indeed."
—EDWARD YOUNG

"Generalization no. 1— The secret of happiness is to want neither too much nor too little.
"Generalization no. 2— No one can master this secret, under the age of 39."   —LYTTON STRACHEY

"Philosophers and poets may be as cute as they like about middle age, but the question remains, 'What begins at forty?'
"Your laugh lines turn to wrinkles, the dimples in your knees and elbows fill in, you need glasses to read billboards, you find yourself listening to every word of the commercials on motel management and when you at last figure your teen-agers are old enough to be told about sex, you've forgotten what it is you weren't supposed to tell them until they were old enough to be told."
—ERMA BOMBECK

♦ ♦ ♦ ♦

What's in a Number?

"When women pass thirty, they first forget their age; when forty, they forget that they ever remembered it."
—NINON DE L'ENCLOS

"Thirty-five is a very attractive age; London society is full of women who have of their own free choice remained thirty-five for years."   —OSCAR WILDE

"That's the trouble with us. We number everything. Take women, for example. I think they deserve to have more than twelve years between the ages of twenty-eight and forty."   —JAMES THURBER

"I shall always remain between 30 and 40, because I think the 25 years between 30 and 40 are the most interesting in any woman's life." —CONSTANCE BENNETT

"Women are most fascinating between the age of thirty-five and forty after they have won a few races and know how to pace themselves. Since few women ever pass forty, maximum fascination can continue indefinitely." —CHRISTIAN DIOR

"The Grecian ladies counted their age from their marriage, not from their birth." —HOMER

"Allow me to put the record straight. I am 46 and have been for some years past." —ERICA JONG

"I am just turning forty and taking my time about it." —HAROLD LLOYD, at 77

"Even though forty is only a symbolic number, somehow, when you reach that age, you can't fool yourself into thinking you're still a kid. I know that if I tried to be a kid, I'd feel more than a little foolish." —ART GARFUNKEL

"I'm doing more now onstage than when I was 20, but it can't go on forever." —MICK JAGGER

"Even though I'm forty years old and I'm getting a little gray hair on my head, I'm still growing. You're being born a little bit every day." —JOHNNY CASH

"The best years are the forties: after fifty a man begins to deteriorate. But in the forties he is at the maximum of his villainy."   —H. L. Mencken

"I am resolved to grow fat, and look young till forty, and then slip out of the world with the first wrinkle and the reputation of five-and-twenty."   —John Dryden

"The first forty years of life give us the text; the next thirty supply the commentary."   —Arthur Schopenhauer

"The next 40 years, I'm not busting my hump and worrying about money."   —Phil Esposito

"Whatever changes I'm going through because I'm 40 I'm thankful for, because they give me some insight into the madness I've been living in all my life."
                              —John Lennon

"If you know what a cowcatcher is you're over forty."
                              —Jerome Beatty, Jr.

"No matter how long he lives, no man ever becomes as wise as the average woman of forty-eight."
                              —H. L. Mencken

"When I was in my twenties, I was pretty sure I'd be dead by age forty. . . . Forty was the dreaded beginning of middle age and fifty was when you finally got it all together just in time to turn sixty and die."
                              —Willie Nelson

"I always did believe I would die before I was forty . . ."
                              —Little Richard

"Men over forty are no judges of a book written in a new spirit."   —Ralph Waldo Emerson

"Every man over forty who acquiesces is a scoundrel."
—GEORGE BERNARD SHAW

"At forty, one counts carefully one's remaining vitality and resources."
—F. SCOTT FITZGERALD

♦ ♦ ♦ ♦

The Fear of 40

"Is there, after forty, any alternative to bridge?"
—H. G. WELLS

"At the age of forty I thought, 'Old age lies in wait for me at the bottom of my mirror; it's inevitable; it will take hold of me.' "
—SIMONE DE BEAUVOIR

"The terror of turning forty is not that you are midway through life; it is that suddenly, irrevocably, you are half-dead. You begin to look back over what now, as you contemplate it, seems to be a very long stretch of time and ask yourself, 'Just what was all that about?' "
—DIGBY DIEHL

"I just turned forty, and I'm realizing my finiteness. It's a cliché, but it really did come home to me that I don't have forever with the people I love.

"[It is] really hard to be older. There are doors that close for every door that opens. . . . We don't have much acceptance of aging, period, and it's more difficult to be a woman."
—CYBILL SHEPHERD

"Age has been a terrific phobia with me. When I was 30, I felt that the next day I was going to be 40. When I was 40, I felt that the next day I was going to be 50."
—JAMES THURBER

"To reach forty not only gives you to pause, but makes you wonder if you can start up again; it is a damned disturbing sensation. . . . At forty, you can look back a long way and see how you got here, although it's too late to do anything much about it." —ROBERT M. YODER

"Forty years of age. . . . I contemplate the years gone by, the horrible years, I spend my time reflecting on the brevity of life, nothing else; and my will continues to rust away." —CHARLES BAUDELAIRE

"For a woman, [forty] is torture, the end. I think turning forty is miserable. . . ." —PRINCESS GRACE OF MONACO

"I tell you old and young are better than tired middle-aged, nothing is so dead dead-tired, dead every way as middle-aged, have we the guts to make a noise while we are still young before we get middle-aged, tired middle aged." —GERTRUDE STEIN

"I don't want to become a pathetic rock-'n'-roller and take a slow climb down, like a lot of people do. . . . When I'm 40, I don't want to be charging around the countryside doing concerts. I'd rather retire gracefully—get out when people least expect it." —ELTON JOHN

"How does looking at 40 feel? Let's not lie about it. For a sensible, bright, and self-sufficient single woman, it feels like sliding into hot slime." —JOAN FRANK

♦ ♦ ♦ ♦

"Once you get past the fear of being responsible, it feels good. At forty, it suddenly seems unattractive to be a boy and very attractive to be a man." —PAUL SIMON

"Finally, at forty, one should begin to set one's house in order. What's worth keeping should be made as good as possible. What ought to be suppressed should be dropped." —GORE VIDAL

"Human nature being what it is, expecting a man past forty to stop casting appraising and covetous eyes at young girls is like asking the tariff to stay put or grapefruit juice to stay out of your eye. You won't get very far." —LETITIA PRESTON RANDALL

"After four-and-twenty a man is seldom taken by surprise; at least, not till he is past forty; and then, the fear of being too late sometimes renovates the eagerness of his first youth." —FANNY BURNEY

"From forty till fifty a man is at heart either a stoic or a satyr." —SIR ARTHUR W. PINERO

"It is all over for the man of forty who is held in aversion." —CONFUCIUS

"You, men of 40, and you women of 39 who are really 40—what's all this I hear about your being middle-aged? Why, you're just kids—slightly obese kids—that's all! . . .

"You think that just because you gasp for breath when you lean over to fasten your skates, you are no good any longer. Poppycock! Life is just beginning for you, if you only knew it—and if Life only knew it." —ROBERT BENCHLEY

"Middle age: when you're sitting at home on Saturday night and the telephone rings and you hope it isn't for you." —OGDEN NASH

"When I look around me, I'm beginning to think a lot of guys I see nowadays are 40 before they develop a great deal of emotional maturity. I think we men mature a little later in life." —TED DANSON

"I think a woman of forty has another forty years ahead to have a lovely life. Let's face it—you can have a terrible life when you're thirty. The secret is to seize the moment now—and make the most of it." —BARBARA WALTERS

"I've come to grips with what my career will be like, what my life is all about. I'm not going to jump from one year to another, from one job to another, the way I used to do. . . . Whatever, I'm thinking in terms of making as much money as I can. . . . I used to think much less of the future than I do now." —CHEVY CHASE

♦ ♦ ♦ ♦

Grouches

"Men's minds, they say, ossify after forty." —ADOLPH S. OKO

"A man of forty is either a fool or a physician." —OLD PROVERB

"Women of forty always fancy they have found the fountain of youth, and that they remain young in the midst of the ruins of their day." —ARSÈNE HOUSSAYE

"I'm not terribly pleased at being forty. It came as a jolt. Partly because I feel I should be so much more grown-up and wiser about the world than I am. At forty you should know a lot, shouldn't you? It was the same when I turned thirty. I thought: I'm a woman. I should have

Reprinted with permission from Hallmark Cards, Inc.

acquired a lot more knowledge than I have. But I've resigned myself to it now."

—PRINCESS GRACE OF MONACO

"There are no pitfalls for the woman over forty. . . . There's only one possibility for her, and that is she will end life on a sofa with hot bottles at head and feet."

—DJUNA BARNES

"From middle age on, everything of interest is either illegal, immoral, or fattening."   —ALEXANDER WOLLCOTT

"The wages of a chocolate sundae at sixteen is only the price listed on the menu. But a sundae at forty-five is a double chin and a spare tire around the waist."

—CONSTANCE FOSTER

"When a man is past forty and does not become a crook, he is either feebleminded or a genius."   —LIN YUTANG

"On passing his fortieth year, any man of the slightest power of mind—any man, that is, who has more than the sorry share of intellect with which nature has endowed five-sixths of mankind—will hardly fail to show some trace of misanthropy."   —ARTHUR SCHOPENHAUER

"Whoever is not a misanthrope at forty can never have loved mankind."   —NICOLAS CHAMFORT

"I have a troubled past, a troubled present, and a troubled future."   —WOODY ALLEN at 40

"He that is not handsome at twenty, nor strong at thirty, nor rich at forty, nor wise at fifty, will never be handsome, strong, rich, or wise."   —GEORGE HERBERT

"Before he knows where he is, a man finds himself floundering in the perilous forties. He is now that baldish, stout person whom twenty years before he jeered at when he saw him dancing, a little out of breath, with girls who might be his daughters. He is now the gentleman in the Rolls-Royce, smoking a long cigar, whom he used to outdrive at golf by thirty yards and who wilted not a little towards the end of the second round. Yesterday, he was a young man, and today he drinks lithia water."
                    —W. SOMERSET MAUGHAM

"It is in the thirties that we want friends. In the forties we know they won't save us any more than love did."
                    —F. SCOTT FITZGERALD

"Your path stretches so smooth, so gracious. There are no more ways for you to make a fool of yourself; you have assembled the complete set. There are no more mistakes; you have made them all. There are, for you, only ease and fulfillment and tenderness. And you did not work to gain them. These are given to you as gifts for this, your happiest birthday." —DOROTHY PARKER

"I am an old man, an old man. I am already forty-six." —LENIN

"My coevals flatter me by assuring me that I am still the same springy kid and that I haven't changed a whit. I know better; I am beginning to examine with considerable interest those advertisements of lean, gray-haired fishermen whipping a trout stream with no impaired faculties and a tidy income of $175 a month. I also find that if I bend over rapidly three thousand times, I have to pause to recover my breath." —S. J. PERELMAN

"Middle age is when you've met so many people that every new person you meet reminds you of someone else." —OGDEN NASH

"A man has more character in his face at forty than at twenty—he has suffered longer." —MAE WEST

"Today is my forty-third birthday. I have thus long passed the peak of life where the waters divide." —ESIAS TEGNÉR

"I wouldn't go back in time for anything in the world. When I was younger, I was defenseless . . . fearful that I couldn't live up to other people's standards. Now I'm stronger, able to take care of myself, enjoying my work and my time on this planet." —ELLEN BURSTYN

"Any man worth his salt has by the time he is forty-five accumulated a crown of thorns, and the problem is to learn to wear it over one ear." —CHRISTOPHER MORLEY

"By age 40, almost everyone has experienced enlarging sadnesses, such as the deaths of loved ones; enriching delights, such as introducing a child to Huckleberry Finn; deepening astonishments, such as contemplation of this fact of life: physically, you ain't what you used to be. Every instant, every cell in your body is changing. This 40-year-old jumble of space and electricity is not the jumble it was at 30. Our continuity is more in our memories than in our physiologies." —GEORGE F. WILL

"We don't understand life any better at forty than at twenty, but we know it and admit it." —JULES RENARD

"When you get to be forty-five, the only thing you really want is another shot at the ten years since you were thirty-five, or better, at the fifteen years since you were thirty." —JAMES THURBER

"I'm in my forties now. My forties! And maybe I'm only just coming to understand what that character [Mary Richards] felt. I'm doing today what most people do at 23, and I'm having fun with my life as opposed to simply concentrating at work." —MARY TYLER MOORE

♦ ♦ ♦ ♦

Age Versus Youth

"At twenty forty is charming; at forty twenty." —GEORGE MEREDITH

"Twenty thinks forty is stale and commonplace. Forty thinks twenty is foolish and dumb. In a way, they're both right." —RUBE GOLDBERG

"Children despise their parents until the age of forty, when they suddenly become just like them—thus preserving the system." —QUENTIN CREWE

"I suppose that up until the age of 39, 40 seems old." —HELEN LAWRENSON

"Setting a good example for your children takes all the fun out of middle age." —WILLIAM FEATHER

"I'm neither young nor old. I'm midway between the two. I'm something being formed. I'm an aging process—a rose that has nothing sprouting forth, but just opens and blows." —ANTOINE DE SAINT-EXUPÉRY

"In the 1950's, when time was creeping along so slowly, people who were in their forties were really quite old and decrepit. I can remember this quite distinctly. Now that time has speeded up so much, however, people who are now in their forties and even in their fifties seem very youthful and energetic." —CHARLES OSGOOD

"By the time people are forty, they no longer feel at all physically superior to anyone twenty so they satisfy themselves feeling superior to those fifty. This continues for life. When my mother was eighty, she spoke in disparaging terms of several women who were still playing bridge at ninety." —ANDY ROONEY

◆ ◆ ◆ ◆

"My notion of a wife at forty is that a man should be able to change her, like a banknote, for two twenties." —DOUGLAS JERROLD

"Up to forty a woman has only forty springs in her heart. After that age she has only forty winters."
—Arsène Houssaye

"A lively writer— I cannot recollect his name—asks what business women turned of forty have to do in the world."
—Mary Wollstonecraft

"Forty is more than a birthday. It is the age when the effort to look young turns from a hobby into a career; when the illusion of being young releases the alleged siren and represents the last stand of sex appeal. It is the flirtatious age, the age of the exaggerated flutter of the eyes, the gooey note in the voice. . . . Forty is the age when the triumph of mind over matter begins."
—Rae Norden Sauder

"I never intend to look a day over 28, but it's going to cost Donald a bundle." —Ivana Trump, *who allegedly underwent a surgical makeover at age 40*

"I'm between 29 and danger—that's how I'm looking at it. . . . Now when I'm reaching the end of my rope, I just tie a knot and hang on." —Tammy Wynette

"When I was 27, I felt like a pebble on the beach. Now I feel like the whole beach." —Shirley MacLaine

"I decided it was time to do some serious growing up."
—Bette Midler

"Where I come from, the smart guys look for the women with maturity and experience. It's the difference between jug and vintage wine." —Rita Moreno

"I realize I can't compete with the eighteen-year-olds in Malibu any more. I don't try to. But I do know a few things they don't know. The secret is not to get lazy and panic." —ALI McGRAW

"I am in my prime. . . . I'm not so anxious about my age. I was—and it still hits me sometimes. I guess I really went through it when I was 32 or 34. I don't mind being an adult woman. I find it interesting. Of course, it might be a problem if it didn't interest anyone else. I can't just do monologues, after all. Anyway, I find more and more people are turning 40." —BIBI ANDERSSON

"Youth in a woman is frightfully overrated. . . . Mercifully, one grows up. One's responses to life at forty are infinitely more tender. Tender, tender, tender! Don't you see?" —MRS. LATHAM, in *Forty Carats*, adapted by Jay Presson Allen

◆ ◆ ◆ ◆

Optimists

"You're never too old to do what you want if you're fat enough." —GEORGE FOREMAN

"At 40 a man has come of age. He has more polish, charm, poise—and more money." —MAE WEST

"What a man does before forty does not matter." —HENRY FORD

"I love men in their prime—which is 40 to 55. That's when they're self-assured; their face is craggy, without that piece of rooster skin hanging. I don't like blonds; I like dark men who look a little beaten-up. He could be the Mafia, but he *does* own Standard Oil." —JOAN RIVERS

"I'm happier now than I've been in many, many years. . . . Life just gets better and better, health permitting. I know so many wonderful people my age, especially women, juicy, bright, not cosmetically involved women. I don't know why people go to the trouble of trying to make the years disappear." —ALI MCGRAW

"By the time we reach 40, we realize that most of our inhibitions are foolish." —JANET DAILEY

"It's nothing that really worries me. If it was just down to me, I think I would hardly notice it. Plus, with the kids, I don't particularly want to be youthful. I want to be a father. Being youthful, rock-'n'-roll, I've done that for so long. I'm ready to move over to a bit of maturity." —PAUL MCCARTNEY

"The middle-aged are not expected to swim, so we can float on our backs for as long as we like." —ALAN BRIEN

"At forty, you begin to know what's important and what's ridiculous. . . . At forty, you have some clues as to who the hell you are. I think the most attractive thing about a woman is the sense of past experience—the hard knocks and the exhilarations. . . . I have more to give, more sympathy, more understanding. The thought of my being thirty again puts me to sleep." —BARBARA HOWAR

"Forty isn't fatal." —LINDA EVANS

"It's been very liberating for me to admit my age. People don't look at me like I'm a little girl anymore. It's the best thing to happen to me. I think a woman really becomes her most attractive in her late 30s and in her 40s. When I look at pictures of myself when I was younger, I like the way I look now better. There's some character in my face that has come from living. I think it's too bad that so many women want to get rid of that character with plastic surgery." —SUSAN ANTON

"Being forty doesn't bother me. I think it's because I'm very happy. I've discovered that you really can get wiser and avoid the mistakes of your youth." —JANE FONDA

"People who hide their age, that's sick. I'm very happy to be 42. I can't wait to be 55. I'm gonna be an awesome diva by then." —PATTI LaBELLE

"Oh, shit—I wanna be there! When somebody says to me—which they do like every five years—'How does it feel to be over the hill,' my response is, 'I'm just heading up the mountain.' I want to get a look at the promised land, so don't bother me with the hill—on it, up it, over it, whatever. There are more important things." —JOAN BAEZ

◆ ◆ ◆ ◆

"When you reach 40, you may still have a fear of pain, but you also have the knowledge that you'll survive it." —MARIETTE HARTLEY

"I don't understand crooners; I don't know why a woman's hat should cost four times as much as a man's when it is one-quarter as large; I can't see any reason for whiskers; I make the same mistakes over and over at bridge; I can't figure out why they make you stop at a traffic light when there's no traffic; I don't know how to eat spaghetti; I can't enjoy riding in a rumble seat; and I don't know the reason for the Depression. So I ask, crying in the wilderness of doubt and confusion, where is all that mature knowledge that comes to a man when he is well over forty? . . . How can I be so smart when I still wear bow ties?" —RUBE GOLDBERG

"After forty, most of us lose interest in changing our work, our play, our domicile, and our friends. More and more we prefer to be let alone." —WALTER B. PITKIN

"Basically, this is your opportunity to do what you've always wanted to do. Forget what 'the world,' the neighbors, or even your family expect of you. Take that vacation you've been talking about. Start piano lessons. Go back to college and get your degree. Don't build a bookcase if you hate carpentry—go to the beach instead. Who says you must go to the Smiths' dinner party? Who says you must make a pile of money?" —DR. MARTIN SYMONDS

"People whose grandparents were all long-lived and lived with the family, shoot each other before they are forty." —ROBERT BENCHLEY

" 'George,' he said, when the waiter walked over for his empty glass, 'I will be forty-one next November.' 'But that's not old, sir, and that's a long way off,' said George. 'No, it isn't,' he said. 'It's almost here. So is forty-two and forty-three and fifty, and here I am trying to be—do you know what I'm trying to be, George? I'm trying to be happy. . . . But you see, George, I am an analyzer. I am also a rememberer. I have a pocketful of old used years. You put all those things together and they sit in a lobby getting silly and old.' " —JAMES THURBER

"The true meaning of turning forty: a gentle reminder that you never did all those things you planned to do." —JOHN D. BOYD

JACK BENNY:
FOREVER 39

"No matter how often I tell people I'm thirty-nine some of them refuse to believe I'm that old."

—Jack Benny

On an early television episode of "The Jack Benny Show," in the mid-fifties, Jack Benny dressed himself in a silly and not terribly effective disguise and pretended to be a contestant on the popular quiz show "You Bet Your Life," hosted by guest star (and real host) Groucho Marx. Naturally Jack defeated the other contestants and reached the jackpot round, only to be confronted with the following embarrassing question: "What," asked Groucho innocently, "is the real age of that famous comedian, Jack Benny?"

Jack hesitated, looking helplessly at the audience. As the seconds ticked off the clock, he grew more and more obviously discomfited, wondering whether he should tell the truth and win the $3,000 prize, or preserve his vanity. At last, just before the buzzer sounded, he answered hopefully, "Thirty-nine," and lost the jackpot.

Later, after Jack had shed his disguise, Groucho asked, "Jack, you had a chance to win the jackpot. Why didn't you give your right age?"

"Groucho," Jack replied, "where else can you buy twenty-two years of life for just three thousand dollars?"

Jack Benny was not always 39 years old. In real life, he turned 40 on February 14 (Valentine's Day), 1934; by that time, his Sunday evening radio show sat atop the ratings as the most popular program in North America. Shortly after his 50th birthday ("If fifty is only middle-aged," Jack once wondered, "how come you don't see too many hundred-year-old men?"), Benny's writers decided to have him fib about his age on the air. Originally they made him pretend to be 36 years old so that he could announce proudly to a nurse that "I'm thirty-six—a perfect thirty-six."

So 36 he remained for three years, until he hit 37 with considerable public fanfare. "Thirty-seven is such a nice age I've decided to hold it over for another year," Jack told reporters, and 38 seemed to last even longer, until at least he reached the magic age of 39.

> After he was "thirty-nine" a few years, he did a radio program on which his birthday came up and the script called for him to turn "forty," a time of great unhappiness for him. However, just before the end of the program, a telegram came from his sister in Waukegan telling him that there had been a mistake on his birth certificate which they just discovered and that actually he had been born a year later, so he had just turned "thirty-nine." —IRVING A. FEIN

And there Jack Benny remained, poised forever on the edge of turning 40.

The running joke about his age became such an ingrained part of American culture that newspapers could run weather reports that announced simply, MERCURY REACHES BENNY, as if no further explanation were necessary. In a campaign to sell a low-cost insurance plan known as "Americare 39," the American Republic Life Insurance Company paid Jack $500,000 a year for the use of his name and image in its advertisements for "life insurance at Jack Benny prices." ("Gee," Jack wondered wistfully in one ad, "why wasn't this available the first time I was thirty-nine?")

Jack and Mary and Gracie and I were going to dinner one night and Gracie asked Mary, "Is Jack really thirty-nine?" and Mary said, "Ridiculous." Then she asked, "Is he really cheap?" and Mary said, "Ridiculous." And then she asked, "And how is his sex life?" and Mary said, "Ridiculous!"
—GEORGE BURNS

In early February 1954, Jack wrote an article for *Collier's* magazine in which he offered his personal tips on "How to Avoid Being 40":

1. Before your fortieth birthday keep circulating the story that you're thirty-nine. If people hear it often enough they'll believe it for years.

2. When in the company of younger people, ask their advice on everything. Pretty soon they'll begin to believe they're older than you are.

3. Stay slim. Thin people always look younger. Connie Mack is ninety-one, but he's so slender nobody figures him to be more than eighty-eight.

4. If you have to spend any money, do it grudgingly. People will think you're saving up for your old age instead of entering it. . . .

5. Avoid reminiscing about the past. If the name Lincoln should come up in your conversation, be sure that it's the car you're talking about and not the President.

6. Lastly, don't worry about your fortieth birthday. Remember, it will soon be over, and it will never happen again.

HAPPY BIRTHDAY (PARTIES AND PRESENTS)

Fortieth-birthday parties traditionally have provided the opportunity for a special and uniquely agonizing type of rite-of-passage celebration, usually with an "oh, no, here-we-go-over-the-hill" motif. Here, at last, is your chance to trot out those perennially popular trick inextinguishable birthday cake candles that continue to blaze away under the strongest puffs, until the guest of honor is wheezing and gasping for breath—though I would recommend using less than 40 of them for an indoor party, unless you want to notify your local fire department ahead of time. Sentimental types who frown on such lighthearted frolics may want to display memorabilia (boy, that word sure makes you sound like an antique, doesn't it?) from each decade of the person's life—or even something from each year, if you have a particularly spacious party room.

Gifts for 40th birthdays typically range from the out-rageous to the tasteless, and beyond to the bizarre. If you don't mind seeing your present go up in smoke, you may want to hire a skywriter to publish a public declaration of love to your spouse across the heavens, as Yoko Ono did for John Lennon's 40th birthday. Foam-rubber tombstones are definitely inappropriate (save them for 50), though bouquets of black roses—the latest fashion in Southern California—are certainly acceptable, so long as their meaning is not misunderstood. One distraught woman phoned the florist after her husband received such a bouquet, terrified that the Mafia had sent the flowers as a death threat.

The most creative gift idea, however, comes from a woodworker in Windsor, Massachusetts, who sells via mail order personalized "Life Coffins" for any 40-year-olds who are looking to the future (far into the future), beyond any mere midlife crisis. "Buying a coffin now can help begin a process of education and self-acceptance," he claims. "By seeing your coffin every day, you will be reminded of the preciousness of your physical life. This perspective on your daily hassles can bring a feeling of celebration of the miracle of your life rather than merely surviving."

Well, perhaps. Available in cherry, oak, or knotty eastern white pine (cherry and oak, however, do cost extra), the coffin is made from kiln-dried lumber and sealed—except for the top lid, of course—with a water-based, nontoxic (as if it mattered) glue. Customers must supply the proper dimensions for the receptacle—their height in bare feet, plus four inches—and should be advised that the standard life coffin is only 28" wide. While awaiting one's passage into the promised land, one might employ the coffin as a bookcase for those cherished volumes of immortal literature, or as a convenient wine rack (twelve-bottle stackable units fit nicely inside).

"People do approach milestones in their own particular way. On my husband's fortieth birthday, he locked himself in his bedroom with a copy of *Playboy* magazine and made an obscene phone call to Ted Mack."

—ERMA BOMBECK

"As the day approached, practically everyone I met told me a Turning Forty story. One guy was convinced that he would die on his fortieth birthday and had gathered all his friends for a twenty-four-hour deathwatch/drinking spree. Several men, for different reasons, had spent the Big Birthday in bed. One of them hired two prostitutes to try a few things he had never done before. Another friend settled down on the eve of his fortieth to read *Passages*, a book he had been told would offer insight into his problems. He opened the paperback version only to discover to his horror that the page was a blur. He spent his birthday at the ophthalmologist being fitted for reading glasses."

—DIGBY DIEHL

"The morning of my fortieth birthday, I awoke with the same old cold dread of unavoidable doom that Marie Antoinette must have felt when she awoke and knew that this was the day that she was to be guillotined."

—MARY BARD

"I went to Newton Ferrers for my 40th birthday. I got few presents and no letters."

—EVELYN WAUGH

"Come, then, a song, a song! Happy birthday to you, happy birthday to you, happy birthday, poor bastard, happy birthday to-o-o you!

"This is it, you know. This is the one that does it. You have said farewell to the thirties for the tenth and last

Doonesbury is syndicated internationally by Universal Press Syndicate. Copyright © 1989 by G. B. Trudeau. All rights reserved.

time. Now you face it, baby. Now you take it smack in the teeth, baby. Quote baby unquote."

—DOROTHY PARKER

"On my fortieth birthday, my family chipped in and bought me a tennis racket. I don't wish to sound ungrateful, but this is like buying the Pope a Mouseketeer beanie.

" 'When are you going to use it?' the kids kept clamoring.

" 'When it snows and I get another racket to put on the other foot,' I said."

—ERMA BOMBECK

"If the months leading up to the 40th birthday had a sound track, it would be the shrieking dissonance of 'Psycho.' Models and movie stars are suddenly much younger than you. Your friends' kids are grown. The bag boy at the supermarket calls you 'ma'am.' It's jarring, it's astonishing, it's vaguely sickening, and so what. The brutal truth is you're on your own as you go over the falls of 40. No one can save you. The culture doesn't care. It's busy selling things."

—JOAN FRANK

♦ ♦ ♦ ♦

Jacqueline Kennedy Onassis wins the *Turning 40* award for receiving the most expensive 40th birthday presents. Celebrating the big day less than a year after her marriage to Aristotle Onassis, she received first a dozen red roses, flown in from Athens to the Onassis island hideaway on Skorpios; then Ari presented her with jewelry reportedly worth at least one million dollars: a 40-carat diamond ring from Van Cleef in Paris, ruby earrings, and a Zolotas bracelet fashioned in the shape of a goat (for Capricorn, his birth sign). The accompanying festivities continued on and off the yacht *Christina* and the mainland for at least two days and nights; at one party in a nightclub near

Athens, Jackie wore a solid gold chain belt bearing her own astrological sign, a lion.

Lord Horatio Nelson, the famed British admiral of the Napoleonic era, received a more enduring and public tribute when he turned 40. "The preparations of Lady Hamilton [Nelson's lover] for celebrating my birthday tomorrow, are enough to fill me with vanity," the admiral wrote gleefully from Naples, where the fleet was stationed, to his wife far away in England. "Every ribbon, every button, has 'Nelson,' etc. The whole service is marked 'H[oratio] N[elson] Glorious 1st of August [the anniversary of the Battle of Trafalgar]! '—Songs and Sonetti are numerous beyond what I ever could deserve."

In Nelson's honor, the British government authorized the addition of a new verse to the anthem, "God Save the King":

> *Join we in Great Nelson's name,*
> *First on the rolls of Fame,*
> *Him let us sing.*
> *Spread we his fame around,*
> *Honour of British ground,*
> *Who made Nile's shores resound,*
> *God Save the King.*

Andy Warhol spent his 40th birthday in bed, watching television and reading while recuperating from gunshot wounds inflicted by a sometime actress and fanatical feminist who apparently had embarked upon a campaign to eradicate male human beings from the face of the earth.

Napoleon celebrated his 40th birthday at his château in Schönbrunn in Austria, having recently won the battle of Wagram—the final great victory of his reign. To ingratiate themselves with their new emperor, the citizens of Vienna commemorated the event by illuminating all the windows of the city with candles and lamps, a dazzling display in Europe's most charming city. Napoleon chose the occasion to announce that he intended to erect a Temple of Glory—a 180-foot-high obelisk—at the approach to the Pont Neuf in Paris, in honor of the military conquests of the Grande Armée.

Unfortunately, the festivities were marred by a fatal accident at Schönbrunn, when a soldier who had been helping to prepare the spectacular fireworks exhibition planned for the emperor's birthday accidentally set a rocket fuse on fire and, panic-stricken, tossed the sputtering missile into an artillery storeroom filled with gunpowder. The ensuing explosion killed eighteen men and wounded seven more.

◆ ◆ ◆ ◆

"My fortieth birthday, now that I think of it, was not very wonderful either. . . . For a birthday treat [my boyfriend] took me on a tour of topless bars, then much in vogue but not, really, the most tactful choice for a woman newly forty."
                                                    —ALICE ADAMS

"I guess I had a [40th] birthday that August, the eighteenth. If anyone attempted to say, 'Happy birthday,' I growled."
                                                    —SHELLEY WINTERS

"Whoever decided that a birthday was an occasion for a party celebrating the day? I can understand kids having birthday parties, but no one past thirty thinks a birthday is any occasion for celebrating. . . . You don't catch anyone approaching middle age, with a birthday six months past, saying, 'I'm forty-two and a half' or 'I'm almost forty-three.' Right up until midnight of the day before the birthday, that person's going to be filling out forms and answering the question with 'forty-two.' Never mind the details."
                                                    —ANDY ROONEY

"Rochester volunteered to contribute the cake, provided I paid for the forty candles. I told him that was satisfactory. I knew I wouldn't have to buy forty candles. I could get ten and cut them in quarters." —JACK BENNY

♦ ♦ ♦ ♦

SONGS FOR A 40TH BIRTHDAY

A Pirate Looks at Forty—Jimmy Buffett

Touch of Gray—Grateful Dead

You've Been a Good Old Wagon, Daddy, But You Done Broke Down—Carolyn Hester

Starting Over—John Lennon

Golden Years—David Bowie

It's Never Too Late—George Blanda

The Real Life—John Cougar Mellencamp

Middle Age Crazy—Johnny Paycheck

Nick of Time—Bonnie Raitt

Nobody Loves a Fairy When She's Forty—Arthur W. D. Henley

Get Over It—Eagles

♦ ♦ ♦ ♦

Guests to Hollywood director/actor Rob Reiner's 40th birthday party were requested to bring a tape or film clip of their most embarrassing theatrical work. Bruno Kirby, for instance, brought a copy of the rightly notorious 1973 bomb "The Harrad Experiment," an early venture in on-screen nudity in which every conceivable ploy was used to display as much skin as possible. But the hands-down winner for the worst performance in a supporting role was Reiner himself, for his appearance as a long-haired hippie singing a duet of *Blowin' in the Wind* with Jim Nabors on the late "Gomer Pyle, U.S.M.C." television show.

For his 40th birthday, Lyndon Baines Johnson received his first nomination to the United States Senate, courtesy of an extremely narrow victory in a Texas Democratic primary election. One day before the election, Johnson celebrated his birthday at a giant campaign rally in San Antonio. "You know, life begins at forty," he shouted to the raucous throng as the assembled bands played *Happy Birthday*, "and I hope to be the next junior Senator when I am forty years and one day old." Johnson won the ensuing election, though some critics claim L.B.J. and his wealthy supporters stole the vote outright.

On his 40th birthday, the Marquis de Sade was lodged in prison outside of Paris on accusations of immoral conduct. He was later transferred to the Bastille, where he remained for more than a decade.

For composer Richard Wagner's 40th birthday, his friends in the city of Zurich sponsored the first "Wagner Festival" in history, featuring an all-star aggregation of musicians and singers performing selections from his works, particularly *Rienzi*, *Tannhauser*, and *Lohengrin*. Wagner also received a silver goblet and a laurel wreath —though no money, since the festival ended up nearly 1200 francs in the red.

At his 40th birthday party, veteran blond rocker Tom Petty got together with a few old friends—Bruce Springsteen, Roger McGuinn, Jeff Lynne, Jim Keltner, and the Heartbreakers—and played an impromptu set of rock standards: *Roll Over Beethoven*, *Wipeout*, *Great Balls of Fire*, *Pipeline*, and *Mr. Tambourine Man*.

On Emperor Hirohito's 40th birthday—April 19, 1941 —the Japanese government staged a massive display of modern armed might, the largest military parade in the nation's history. The semiofficial government organ, the *Japan Times and Advertiser*, took the opportunity to announce a "new world order," based upon Japanese domination of the Far East and German control of Europe. Less than eight months later, Japanese armed forces attacked Pearl Harbor.

♦ ♦ ♦ ♦

"The actual event is relatively quiet. (A quiet start for a long, quiet period, sonny.) One day you are thirty, and then, with little or nothing to account for the difference, you are forty. It does not bring general collapse; that idea is overdramatic. You don't wake up on your fortieth birthday with a film on the eyes and a gnarled cane by your bedside. You wake up feeling strange, but no stranger than you felt at thirty-nine. The main difference is emotional; the feeling is about what a race horse must feel when first he sees the dray wagon."

—ROBERT M. YODER

"I dated a 21-year-old girl. Took her to my apartment. Put on a record of Charlie Parker and Dizzy Gillespie playing a Cole Porter tune. She thought it was classical music."   —WOODY ALLEN

"My 40th birthday was the one that was hard for me to adjust to—because other people were having a problem. . . . I was in Europe at the time and I didn't have a problem. But my secretary said my friends did. They'd call up and ask, 'How's she taking it?' . . . 'Is she all right?' I was amused by those calls because I didn't feel that way."   —SHIRLEY MACLAINE

"My birthday was signalised by hearing from Mr. Craik that they have now sold 15,000 *Looking-Glasses*, and have orders for 500 more!"
— CHARLES LUTWIDGE DODGSON (LEWIS CARROLL)

◆ ◆ ◆ ◆

Like Andy Warhol, Elvis Presley passed his 40th birthday in bed, though Elvis had been felled by nothing more serious than the flu and a bad case of grumpiness; later that day, he appeared briefly at a family party his parents and his six-year-old daughter had prepared, then had a private dinner with a female companion. Outside the gates of Graceland, meanwhile, more than 2,000 fans poured their gifts into huge barrels; the Memphis post office was swamped with birthday cards, cakes, telegrams, and more packages. One enterprising pair of Mississippi teenagers boxed themselves up in a carton marked "Russian Wolfhounds" and had themselves delivered to Elvis's mansion, but security guards refused to let the box inside; besides, Elvis already had enough dogs.

Queen Victoria held a formal soirée in St. James' Palace on her 40th birthday. Dressed in three skirts of white tulle, a white satin petticoat, a train of green and silver watered silk, and, around her head, a floral wreath of "Victoria Regina" ornamented with diamonds, feathers, and veils, Her Majesty received an endless procession of princes, princesses, dukes, archbishops, and assorted nobility. Throughout London, the modern gas lights (which had virtually supplanted the old oil lamps) were all blazing away, despite a high wind. Nearby, the Woolwich garrison of more than 4,000 men turned out in a drenching rain to parade, fire a twenty-one-gun salute, and give three cheers for the Queen before they scrambled back under cover; at Portsmouth, the artillery of the fleet, all decked out in bunting, roared its own salute to Her Majesty.

Times change. Wearing a LIFE BEGINS AT FORTY button
(a gift from his sons, Harry and William), Prince Charles
celebrated his 40th birthday by inviting 1,500 underpriv-
ileged youths to a party in the grimy industrial city of
Birmingham, at an abandoned train depot that had been
renovated with money from the Prince's Trust, a group
of charity organizations dedicated to assisting young people in Britain's inner cities. As Charles swayed, a bit stiffly,
to the music of a West Indian steel band, one twenty-
two-year-old observer noted politely that "he moves really
well for his age." Then it was off to Buckingham Palace
for another, more formal party where royalty from Europe
mixed with rock stars such as Elton John and Phil Collins.

◆ ◆ ◆ ◆

"Forty always sounded so important. The Big Four-O. It's
halfway, or more, through life, but I find it so appealing.
I've always wanted to be older."   —ELIZABETH TAYLOR

"I'm doing what I know to the best of my ability. I have
a wonderful life and I manage to make a few pennies.
Show me a man who has any more."
                                                     —RICHARD BURTON

No royal celebration could match the festivities staged
by Richard Burton to mark his wife Elizabeth Taylor's 40th
birthday. Seven years earlier, when Burton had turned
40, Liz had given him a white Oldsmobile wrapped in a
huge red ribbon; after removing the wrappings, Dick
spent the rest of the day showing it off around the studio
lot.

By the time Liz's 40th birthday rolled around, she and
Burton were living in Budapest, where he was starring in
a film version of the life of Bluebeard. Despite public
declarations of mutual devotion, it was not a happy time
for the couple: Burton was drinking far too heavily and

smoking nearly a hundred cigarettes a day; there were rumors of affairs between him and several of his female costars on the set; and Liz had just become a grandmother, courtesy of her eldest son, Michael Wilding, Jr. To paper over their marital woes, Burton planned a lavish extravaganza for Liz's big day. At first he thought of chartering a Concorde SST, to hold "a celestial birthday party while streaking across the heavens at twice the speed of sound." Discarding that notion as impractical, he considered using a jumbo jet instead, stopping at resorts around the world to pick up guests; or perhaps they could all journey across Europe in a luxurious private train, like the old Orient Express.

In the end, Burton settled for a three-day gala in Budapest, a nonstop orgy of lunches, brunches, cocktail parties, and evening dances. Among the 200 guests—some of whom received free first-class air tickets from Burton to attend the affair—were Princess Grace, Michael Caine, Ringo Starr, Raquel Welch, Stephen Spender, and Michael York, though Liz's son Michael refused to attend. Liz spent much of the time showing off her birthday present from Richard, a 300-year-old heart-shaped yellow diamond pendant originally owned by the Shah Jahan (the Indian emperor who built the Taj Mahal) and valued somewhere between $50,000 and $100,000; the words "Eternal love till Death" were inscribed in the gold mounting. "Elizabeth likes it," crowed Burton. "She went over it with a magnifying glass." At least one guest, however, was less than impressed with Liz's glittering appearance on her birthday, comparing her to "a beautiful doughnut covered in diamonds and paint."

Because the Burton–Taylor extravaganza was staged amid the dismal poverty that oppressed most of the Hungarian capital, it generated so much negative publicity that the couple ended up contributing a sum equal to the cost of the party—about $50,000—to the United Nations Children's Fund. "Our love is so deep that I don't give a g—damn what people think or say about us," Liz huffed. Within a year the couple had separated, and two years later they were divorced.

♦ ♦ ♦ ♦

"The 40th is, truth be told, a boring birthday. . . . The 35th is notable as the halfway mark in the Biblical three-score and ten. But the 40th just means middle age, which is so, well, middling." —GEORGE WILL

Some people, of course, refuse to acknowledge their 40th birthday with anything more than a passing nod. Paul McCartney spent the evening at home with his family at his cottage in the Sussex countryside; Oliver Wendell Holmes, too, stayed home and drank champagne with his wife; and Woody Allen spent the day working on the set of his first dramatic film, *The Front*.

Donald Trump saved his friends the trouble of deciding what to get a billionaire for his 40th birthday by scuttling their plans to throw him a surprise 40th birthday party. Claiming that he had no time for such frivolity, or for reflection on the deeper meaning of turning 40, Trump declared that he desired no birthday gifts, either. Instead, Trump spent his birthday in a round of business meetings with architects, lawyers, and bankers. He professed himself satisfied with the first 40 years of his life; "I love what I'm doing," he told one reporter. "I may just now be hitting my stride."

Finally, the *Turning 40* award for the dullest 40th birthday party goes to Edward Albert Christian George Andrew Patrick David, Prince of Wales, Count of Chester, Duke of Cornwall and Rothesay, Count of Carrick, Lord of the Isles, and Grand Master of Scotland and Windsor, later known as King Edward VIII of England and, after his abdication, the Duke of Windsor. Two years before he ascended the throne, Edward—then considered "the world's most-sought bachelor"—turned 40 quietly at Windsor Castle and Fort Belvedere, his favorite residence outside London. His official calendar was kept completely free of engagements; instead, he had only a small family luncheon party at the castle, and then spent the afternoon working in his garden. The only birthday present noted by the press was a specially printed copy of Walter Pitkin's recent bestseller, *Life Begins at Forty*.

Mrs. Wallis Warfield Simpson, who was fast becoming the prince's regular companion, spent the day elsewhere.

♦ ♦ ♦ ♦

"Take it easy, that's all you have to do. Don't fight it. You're the only one who is passionately interested in your age; other people have their own troubles. The matter will probably never come up, unless you fetch it up. After all, how often does the McKinley Inaugural normally creep into the conversation?" —DOROTHY PARKER

♦ ♦ ♦ ♦

And should you choose to spend your 40th birthday quietly at home, watching a movie on your VCR, here are a few appropriate films to look for at your favorite video rental store:

Shirley Valentine (1989)—One of the best, an absolutely marvelous film about a middle-aged English housewife, played by Pauline Collins, who rediscovers not her youth, but the fascinating and vital person she used to be before she fell into a loveless marriage and a dreary everyday suburban routine. "From now on, when I look into the mirror, I'm not going to say, 'Christ, you're 42'; I'm going to say, 'Hey, Shirley, you're only 42—isn't that marvelous?'" A tremendous lift for your spirits.

Robin and Marian (1976)—Sean Connery and Audrey Hepburn as Robin Hood and Maid Marian in their forties. "You reckon it's a good life to have reached forty," Robin tells Little John while they sit in jail at the start of the film. "We're both past it, and look at us." Strips the legend of false glitter and reveals the reality and wonder of age and love beneath it all. Favorite scene: the climactic sword duel between Robin and the equally middle-aged Sheriff of Nottingham, played by Robert Shaw in one of his last roles.

The First Wives Club (1996)—Don't get mad, get even. And have fun and look great while you're doing it. Bette Midler, Goldie Hawn, and Diane Keaton give forty-something women a whole new image.

Slapshot (1977)—Paul Newman, in his late forties, pretending to be a professional ice hockey player. (See Gordie Howe, page 54.)

Eating (1991)—An all-female cast gathers to celebrate the 40th birthday of one of their friends, who decides that she is free to eat anything she chooses on her birthday. Much of the dialogue is improvised; nearly all of it is concerned with the consumption of food and its ultimate appearance on various parts of the characters' anatomy. Favorite line: "I think I'm still looking for a man who could excite me as much as a baked potato."

Forty Carats (1973)—Liv Ullmann plays a 40-year-old divorcée who attracts a 22-year-old admirer while on holiday in Greece. Ullmann (who was really 36 at the time and badly miscast) defends her decision to marry the smitten young man by announcing that "the latest statistics prove that a woman comes into her full sexual flowering at forty,

while a man attains his at twenty." The title comes from the ex-husband's advice to the main character to think of herself as a diamond: "Not years—carats."

Texasville (1990)—The return of the kids from *The Last Picture Show*, now in their forties but not necessarily grown up. Bummer.

Middle-Age Crazy (1980)—Upon reaching his 40th birthday, Bruce Dern feaks out, buys a Porsche and a hip new wardrobe, and abandons his wife, Ann-Margret, to run off with a 20-year-old professional football cheerleader. (See Erskine Caldwell, page 105.)

Over Forty (also known as *Beyond Forty*) (1982)—A group of Canadian childhood friends known as The Gang reunite to reminisce and sing the good old songs.

City Slickers (1991)—Three New Jersey friends, each approaching 40 and facing his own dreaded midlife crisis, take a shot at being cowboys on a cattle drive. Favorite line—Daniel Stern gazing at a beautiful woman: "When I was alive, I would have found her attractive."

None but the Lonely Heart (1944)—Certainly the darkest movie of Cary Grant's illustrious career, and a prime example of the sort of utterly gloomy picture that a man might make in the midst of a midlife crisis. (Grant was 40 when he decided to do this film.)

The Prime of Miss Jean Brodie (1969)—Oscar-winning portrait of a 40ish spinster schoolteacher who counts on her "prime" lasting "until at least fifty." It didn't.

Howard the Duck (1986)—Because if you've made it through 40 years, you're smarter than the people who made this film.

TIME IS ON THEIR SIDE? THE ROLLING STONES TURN 40

Mick Jagger turned 40 in May 1983. Probably. At the time, Matthew Evans, chairman of Faber and Faber, pointed out that Jagger "must be at least 42," because Jagger and Evans, who was 42 himself, were in the same class at the London School of Economics. In any case, Jagger celebrated his 40th birthday in relatively subdued style, taking his girlfriend, Jerry Hall, to a David Bowie concert at Madison Square Garden. Afterward, Jagger mugged for photographers with Bowie, still a relative youngster at 36.

Eight years earlier, Jagger had announced that "I'd rather be dead than sing 'Satisfaction' when I'm 45." Well, Mick is now well past 50, and guess what? Anyway, here is a tribute to the greatest aging rock band in the world.

"I am driven. It's no longer for the money. I always knew I'd be rich. I always thought I was special. . . . I don't want to sound like a spoiled child, but I'm still looking for fulfillment. You've got to fight every inch of the way. Ya know?"   —MICK JAGGER, 1983

"I only want to celebrate my friend's 40th birthday, to rally one and all to do the same. To avoid judging either [Mick's] complexion or his waistline, his future or his past, his genius or his despotism. . . . His talent will be as strong at 50 as it is today at 40 because his ambition is not dependent on his youth, his song writing in the rock genre is not dependent on his own suffering, and his drive to be popular and loved is not dependent on his personal insecurity."   —PETE TOWNSEND, 1983

"I think [Mick's] life—and I have no right to say this—looks pretty dull. It's this way because he doesn't quite know what else to do. It's one of those habits you get into. I got into smack. He got into grand parties—and he got hooked."   —MARIANNE FAITHFULL, 1983

"You know, they're still congratulating the Stones on being together a hundred and twelve years. Whoopee! . . . In the eighties they'll be asking, 'Why are those guys still together? Can't they hack it on their own?' . . . They will be showing pictures of the guy with lipstick wriggling his ass, and the four guys with the evil black makeup on their eyes trying to look raunchy. That's gonna be the joke in the future . . ."   —JOHN LENNON, 1980

"Mick, 47, doesn't look a day over 60."
                    —*People* magazine, 1990

"We're not chucking TVs out of windows anymore. We like to watch them now. . . . I love the band, but there are so many other things. Suddenly, I'm past 40 and there's a lot I want to do before I get past 50."
                    —BILL WYMAN, 1983

"Amazingly enough, in the last few years I've become a happy and contented man. Before that I was too busy and then too strung out. Am I satisfied? Way and above my fantasies." —KEITH RICHARDS, 1983

Shortly before he turned 40, Keith Richards decided to marry longtime girlfriend Patti Hansen. The hastily arranged civil ceremony, held on a hotel terrace overlooking the Pacific Ocean at Cabo San Lucas, Mexico, took place on Keith's 40th birthday, which also happened to be the fourth anniversary of his first date with Patti. "I know that I couldn't have made it without her," Richards said. "Nothing like a good woman. I ain't letting that bitch go." The groom took his vows dressed in a black tuxedo and brand new blue suede shoes; Jagger, the only other Stone present, acted as best man. Afterward, Keith serenaded his new bride with the Hoagy Carmichael standard *The Nearness of You*.

"The Rolling Stones are part of everyone's lives by now. . . . Maybe with 20 years behind our belt, we carry a little bit of extra weight, a little bit of respectability. Maybe we can make the music change with us. Our models, blues players like Muddy Waters, all died in harness. The old guys give you a glimmer of how it can be done. And as for Mick, he's the most contented I've seen him in ages. He still sings louder than anyone else."
—KEITH RICHARDS, 1983

ATHLETES AT

In recent years, the remarkable success of such over-40 professional athletes as Nolan Ryan, George Foreman, Hale Irwin, Carlton Fisk, and Jack Nicklaus has changed the public's perception of what a middle-aged body can do when it is kept in peak condition. (Despite Foreman's cheeseburger and fat-man jokes, he really did train hard for his title bout with Evander Holyfield.)

For all their noteworthy accomplishments, however, these athletes were merely carrying on a tradition that extends from Gordie Howe, who enjoyed his most productive season in the National Hockey League at the age of 41, all the way back to the days of Ty Cobb and Robert "Ruby" Fitzsimmons. The past century has witnessed a gratifying array of 40-year-old Olympic medal winners, race car champions, league-leading hitters, and no-hit pitchers.

Over-40 athletes have shown their mettle in less publicized sports as well. At the age of 41, a runner named

Jack Foster won the Honolulu Marathon with a time of two hours and eleven minutes, one of the most astonishing achievements in the history of competitive running. When a reporter asked him a year later if he had slowed down at all, Foster replied with a straight face, "I don't think so, but I'm concerned that I seem to be stuck around 2:16 and 2:17 when I'm fit."

All of this may serve as inspiration to the rest of us, though of course one should never plunge directly into a program of strenuous exercise without first consulting a physician. You are not Jimmy Connors, and you should not try to be. Certainly recent statistics do indicate that more and more Americans are getting regular exercise; one Louis Harris poll revealed that 46 percent of American men between the ages of 40 and 49 claimed that they participated in outdoor activities such as hiking, fishing, boating, or hunting on a regular basis. Another 23 percent said that they swam regularly; 16 percent played golf; 12 percent were active bicyclers; and 12 percent played baseball or softball, while only 7 percent played football.

Although I admire men like Ryan and Fisk immensely, I can identify more easily with a horse named Forty Something, who ran in the 1991 Kentucky Derby. Although Forty Something had won less than $40,000 in purses and had been beaten by 25 lengths in his only previous race of more than 6 furlongs, his trainer insisted that "he won't be a disgrace." When Forty Something's original rider bowed out at the last minute, owner Sam Morrell hired jockey Andrea Seefeldt to ride him in the Derby. Part of a five-horse parimutuel field, Forty Something went off as a decided longshot, at odds of 16–1.

Nevertheless, he broke quickly and was running well in second place until he reached the three-quarter-mile pole. Then, predictably, Forty Something's legs suddenly gave out and he practically stopped dead in his tracks. "I just had to stay out of everybody's way," Seefeldt explained later. "He backed up so fast, it could have been dangerous." Forty Something struggled to the finish line dead last in the 16-horse field, 37 lengths behind the winner and a full 25 lengths behind the next-to-the-last horse.

♦ ♦ ♦ ♦

"They tell you that things change at forty, but they don't tell you how much." —JOHNNY UNITAS

"I'm going to play as much as I can, as hard as I can, win all I can by the time I'm forty. Then I'm going to go home to El Paso and just sit and count my money. I'm going to have it stacked around the house in bales—not just bundles. And I'm just going to sit there and count it and grin. I ain't going to be out here trying to hack it around and beat the hungry kids." —LEE TREVINO

"I read in the Atlanta paper this week that 46-year-olds don't win Masters. I kind of agreed. I got to thinking. Hmmm. Done, through, washed up. And I sizzled for a while. But I said to myself, I'm not going to quit now, playing the way I'm playing. I've played too well, too long to let a shorter period of bad golf be my last."
—JACK NICKLAUS, after winning the
1986 Masters at age 46

"I think my winning brought people pleasure and some identification with my age group and maybe me. People said, 'Maybe I can do something like that. Maybe I can extend myself.' I could feel it from people. But what's most satisfying is not that I did it at 45, but that I'm a factor again. In that respect, I feel very young."
—HALE IRWIN, after winning the
1990 U.S. Open at age 45

"For thirty-three years, I have operated on the time clock and within the structure and order of the basketball season. It's a serious change coming up. It's as if I have survived the whole cycle, life and death, and here I still am."
—KAREEM ABDUL-JABBAR, 41,
in his last NBA season

"If you are ancient or 45 or 50 and have acquired enough money to go to a ball game, you cannot drive a car on a highway, which is very hard to do after 45, to drive on any modern highway and if you are going to stay home you need radio and television to go along."
—CASEY STENGEL

"When I get to be 40, I'm going to charge people to watch me get out of bed."
—DAVE HERMAN, former New York Jets lineman

"Man, I'll tell you, I wish I never got old. In other jobs, you get old, big deal. In football you get old, you're fired. That's what happened to me. Time got me. Damned time."
—DEACON JONES

"At 44 this year, I'll be the oldest active quarterback in pro football history. I figure I'm 95% as good as I ever was. I still like to hit. I still like to block and tackle, and I don't even mind being knocked on my tail by somebody like Bubba Smith."
—GEORGE BLANDA, after being named
MVP of the NFL at age 43

"When I was forty, my doctor advised me that a man in his forties shouldn't play tennis. I heeded his advice carefully and could hardly wait until I reached fifty to start again."
—HUGO BLACK

"Years ago we discovered the exact point, the dead center of middle age. It occurs when you are too young to take up golf and too old to rush up to the net."

—FRANKLIN P. ADAMS

"I am the Martian man come to life in sports. . . . They don't really have a firm grip if a male body matures between 28 and 32. Now they say maybe it's 35. I might prove they really don't know what the hell they're talking about, and it may not even be until you're 50. I think we're going to redefine what 40-year-olds can do."

—MARK SPITZ

"Age is a myth. Guys in their 40s can be just as strong as younger guys if they work at it. Not in three weeks, but in 33 weeks, maybe. I no longer have the boundaries I once did." —AL OERTER, three-time Olympic shotput gold medal winner

♦ ♦ ♦ ♦

Olympic Medal Winners at 40 or Older

1948—Tebbs Lloyd-Johnson, 48, won the bronze medal in the 50,000 meter walk. Lloyd-Johnson, from Great Britain, is still the oldest person to win any Olympic track and field medal.

1952—Pal Kovacs of Hungary, 40, won a gold medal in the individual sabre competition, fifteen years after winning the world sabre championship.

1960—John Ljunggren of Sweden, 40, won the silver medal in the 50,000 meter walk. Ljunggren had won the gold medal in 1948.

1960—Masao Takemoto, a 40-year-old gymnast, led the Japanese team to a gold medal in the combined gymnastic exercises.

1968—John Braithwaite, a 43-year-old British veterinary surgeon, won the gold medal in trap shooting after missing two of his first 13 shots, and then hitting the last 187 in a row. (Braithwaite had taken up trap shooting because he couldn't stand to shoot real birds and animals and see them suffer.)

♦ ♦ ♦ ♦

"If I failed badly, people would remember me more for trying to make a stupid comeback at 45 than for all the other things I did in hockey. . . . All of a sudden everything began to come easy again. At the start I had to think about what I was doing, but now I was doing it by instinct, just like the old days."

—GORDIE HOWE, MVP of the
World Hockey Association at age 46

"Getting older in racing is definitely a virtue. The older you get, the longer you're in it and the more you realize what it takes to win. You see guys 42, 45 years old racing and winning. I think my generation is going to be more alert, live longer than generations past. So you feasibly could have a race driver reach retirement age 65, and still running strong."　　　　　　　—DARRELL WALTRIP

"If I were fifteen years younger, I'd drop the motion picture industry in a minute . . . if I could drive in competition. But you don't start at forty-three."

—PAUL NEWMAN

"In 1973, I was forty-two years old. That age may be great for a guy practicing law, but for a jockey it's beyond middle-age, especially after twenty-four years of riding. A lot of people who used to greet me with a smile now walked the other way when I came around."

—WILLIE SHOEMAKER

"I'll tell you about age. Age is a number. Being a Muslim, to me age is not important. I don't drink, smoke, move in fast circles. My body is equivalent to that of a 32- or 33-year-old. I can still do the same things I used to do, but I have to plan better. . . . We have to work longer, not harder. Where it used to take four weeks to get into shape, now it takes 12."   —MUHAMMAD ALI at 39

"Age is mind over matter. As long as you don't mind, it don't matter."   —MUHAMMAD ALI, before fight versus
Trevor Berbick in December 1981

"Father time caught up with me. I'm finished. I've got to face the facts. For the first time, I feel that I'm forty years old. I know it's the end; I'm not crazy. . . . I'm happy I'm still pretty. I came out all right for an old man. We all lose sometimes. We all grow old."

—MUHAMMAD ALI, after losing to Trevor Berbick

In April 1991, former heavyweight boxing champion George Foreman made a well-publicized comeback effort at the age of 42. In his title bout against Evander Holyfield, Foreman stirred the imaginations of 40-year-olds everywhere. Despite the skepticism of critics who called him "a forty-two-year-old with jelly doughnuts in his midsection," here was a man who not only refused to hide his age, but professed pride in it.

The Gospel According to George

"After this is over, people are gonna use the words forty, fifty, and sixty with the word potential, and the next future."

"The forty-year-old guys are gonna take over the planet, boy. I'm gonna show the whole world that the age forty or fifty is not a death sentence. We're gonna celebrate, and drink our Geritol, and eat our hamburgers, and walk all over the world, and scare all the gang members."

"I want to be the only guy to stand out by my mailbox waiting for a championship belt that won't fit and a Social Security check at the same time. I'm closer to 50 than I am to 20 and I'm happy about it."

♦ ♦ ♦ ♦

Boxing Champions at Forty

Robert "Ruby" Fitzsimmons—Won light-heavyweight title in a twenty-round fight at the age of 40 (1903), after losing the heavyweight title to Jim Jeffries the previous year. Held light-heavyweight title for two years.

Archie Moore—Won light-heavyweight crown at 39, in 1952. As champion, won nine fights the following year, and held title until it was withdrawn. Lost bids for heavyweight championship at the age of 42 (to Marciano) and 43 (to Patterson).

Sugar Ray Robinson—Won middleweight title at 38 (1958) and held it until after 40th birthday; kept fighting until age 45.

◆ ◆ ◆ ◆

"When you first sign that contract as a kid, they tell you your whole future is ahead of you. But they forget to tell you that your future stops at 35."　　—HAL JEFFCOAT

"After 35, you're on a pass."　　　　—TED WILLIAMS

"I was the first pitcher to pitch two no hitters in the same year, but you know that age robs you of a chance to do that again. To say at 39 you will never cash a paycheck as large again, boy, that would be tough. And you know it's going to happen to a lot of guys playing today."
　　　　　　　　　　　　　　　　—ALLIE REYNOLDS

"I played four games for the Mets in 1965 [at 39]. I was too old. During the year that I managed the Yankees, the skills faded. At that age you have to work at staying sharp. I am not saying the skills I had would have stayed with me if I had played that year and Houk managed. They go no matter what you do. They just go faster on the bench."　　　　　　　　　　　　　　—YOGI BERRA

"I was forty, an age that had sneaked up on me like Big Ed Walsh's spitball; an age when they say a man's inward fires are banked and he's no longer physically capable of satisfying the fans' demands or his own binding sense of pride."　　　　　　　　　　　　　　　　—TY COBB

"In this game, you're constantly having to prove yourself, whether you're 20 or 30 or 40. The problem is, when you get older, you can't afford to go into slumps. When you're young, it's a slump. When you're old, it's just, 'He's too old.' "　　　　　　　　　　　　—DWIGHT EVANS

"Age is meaningless with me."　　　　—PETE ROSE

In 1971, Willie Mays turned in a respectable season at the age of 40, batting .271 with eighteen home runs and sixty-one runs batted in. Writers seemed to derive a particular vicarious satisfaction from watching Mays perform that year; some waxed positively rhapsodic. "The man with the forty years behind him goes to a fly ball in the disguise of youth," wrote Jimmy Cannon. "He suggests an aged falcon who gets to his prey quickly because the act of flight is a spiritual achievement, and not a feat of flapping wings. He is there under the fly ball or running backward or sideways or in because these are familiar routes, and he knows all the shortcuts." And in *Saturday Review*: "Mays moves with the grace of memory, defying time, defying the inexorable erosion of fantasies, defying age itself. . . . It is a good time to be forty—old enough to remember and young enough to believe—a good time to sit in the sun with someone you love."

"Man, I'm almost 40 years old! I can't deal the cards the way I used to when I was 30. I was a power broker in baseball then, but I'm not anymore. I have to take what I'm dealt. . . . Sometimes, when you're 40, you have to sit back and swallow things you don't want to swallow."
—REGGIE JACKSON

"I just couldn't do it at the same level every day, especially with the Coast trips. . . . I'd go into the batting cage and the bat felt like lead. It used to take me a couple of days just to feel normal again—and normal being a forty-year-old guy with bad shoulders who had played 3,000 games. Even eating was a chore."
—CARL YASTRZEMSKI

"Man, I dig being 40 and a great physical specimen. I dig being out there. And I don't want it to end yet. But I can see the end. Yes, I can see it. I'll play this year and try to play next. But no more. I'll play and if August comes around and I'm going like a dog, then it's time to wrap it up." —REGGIE JACKSON

"If you slid into bases head first for 20 years, you'd be ugly too." —PETE ROSE

"I could see a growing and dangerous flaw in me. I was thoroughly tired, no longer baseball-wedded, and I had to have a rest. . . . My reflexes at age forty-one were not good enough to guarantee I wouldn't be beaned by a fastball. . . . My batting eye was almost as dependable as ever, but the legs wouldn't carry me around the garden with speed and timing. Old wounds ached constantly. I literally had to grit my teeth and force myself to run when the chance arose to bunt and beat it out or stretch a single into a double." —TY COBB

"How many 45-year-old guys are cranking up to play opening day? How many are just plain cranking up? Half of them have trouble getting out of bed."
—DALLAS GREEN, after naming 45-year-old Tommy John as the Yankees' 1989 Opening Day starter

"A couple of years ago they told me I was too young to be President and you were too old to be playing baseball. But we fooled them."
—JOHN F. KENNEDY, 45, to Stan Musial, 42

Of course, there have been baseball players who have reached significant career milestones after turning 40. Babe Ruth hit his 700th home run at the age of 40; Don Sutton, Tom Seaver, and Lefty Grove won their 300th games at the age of 41 ("I'm going out for another 300," declared Grove cheerfully); Early Wynn came back for one more year at 43 to win his 300th; Warren Spahn threw his second no-hitter at 40 and, at the age of 42, set the major league record for strikeouts by a lefthander; Hank Aaron passed Babe Ruth's all-time home run record shortly after his 40th birthday; Stan Musial passed Ruth's record for extra base hits at 40; and also at 40, Carl Yastrzemski became the first player ever to amass 3,000 hits and 400 home runs.

And for those players who have turned in excellent individual seasons at the age of 40, we offer the following *TURNING 40* All-Star Team:

C: Carlton Fisk (1989)—hit .293, with 13 home runs; drove in 68 runs.

1B: Cap Anson (1891)—led the American League with 120 runs batted in.

2B: Eddie Collins (1927)—batted .338 for the Chicago White Sox.

SS: Luke Appling (1947)—hit .306, scored 67 runs.

3B: Graig Nettles (1984)—hit 20 home runs, drove in 65 runs.

OF: Ted Williams (1958)—led the American League in batting with a .328 average.

OF: Ty Cobb (1927)—hit .357, scored 104 runs, and drove in 93.

OF: Sam Rice (1930)—batted .349 and scored 121 runs.

RHP: Cy Young (1907)—won 19 games, with earned run average of only 1.99.

RHP: Eddie Plank (1915)—won 21 games, with 2.08 ERA.

LHP: Warren Spahn (1961)—won 21 games, led National League with 21 complete games and an ERA of 3.02.

RP: Gerry Staley (1960)—as relief specialist, appeared in 64 games; won 13 and saved 10, with 2.42 ERA.

RP: Hoyt Wilhelm (1963)—compiled 2.64 ERA and 21 saves; struck out 111.

NOLAN RYAN

Unquestionably, Nolan Ryan accomplished more after the age of 40 than any other player in major league history. When he was 40 and 41, Ryan won strikeout titles in the National League; after moving to the Texas Rangers, he promptly captured the strikeout crown in the American League for the following two years, becoming the oldest player ever to accomplish that feat. By the end of the 1990 season, he had struck out more than 5,200 batters since he broke into the majors 21 years earlier. Then, in 1991, at the age of 44, Nolan Ryan threw the seventh no-hitter of his career—as many as the combined totals of his two closest competitors, Sandy Koufax and Bob Feller.

I interviewed Nolan two weeks before his last no-hitter, to talk about life after 40 in professional baseball:

Q: Nolan, many people, especially in athletics, tend to view the age of forty as a major milestone. When you hit forty, did you stop and wonder why you were still playing this game?

Ryan: Well, no. When I hit forty, I really felt like that was gonna be my last year in baseball, and I've pretty much approached each year since then in the same way. But prior to being forty, I didn't anticipate playing into my forties. I mean, I was as surprised as anyone else that I've been able to continue to participate.

Q: Is it more of a psychological barrier? Do we make too much of it?

Ryan: Well, I didn't make anything of it. It was just another birthday. A lot of people around me made a lot of it. You know, I never gave it any thought, but I never have approached any of my birthdays that way. I've pretty much gone on how I feel more than anything else.

Q: Is it harder to stay in shape now?

Ryan: Yeah, it is. The whole routine is harder. It takes more time, more dedication. Everything revolves around that now, where it didn't before. So your life changes. And I think the longer you continue to do something that requires a lot of physical exertion and conditioning, the older you get, the more you have to give to that, to be able to continue. And that's the toughest part of it now, is the time and commitment that it takes.

Q: But you still do it.

Ryan: Yeah, I'm gonna have to, as long as I continue to put on the uniform. I take pride in being in shape, and I get a lot of satisfaction from having a good workout. And then when you go out and—pitching every fifth or sixth day is a reward for your hard work. Then if you win and have a good game, it's just that much better. But the real reward is getting an opportunity to go out there.

Q: Do sportswriters treat you better, now that you're older?

Ryan: Oh, I wouldn't say they treat you any better, but

I think they probably treat you a little different, same as your teammates, because of the age.

Q: You said in your autobiography that you don't consider yourself a living legend.
Ryan: I don't view myself differently from anybody else.

Q: But you're an inspiration to other men who want to keep on being active.
Ryan: Well, people have indicated that—people in the same age group—that at times I've been an inspiration to them to go ahead and continue to compete or to get back in shape.

Q: There seem to be more athletes over forty in baseball—you, Carlton Fisk, Charlie Hough—than in football or basketball. Is that a result of you guys being in better shape, or is it the game itself?
Ryan: No, I think baseball isn't as demanding on your legs as far as speed and quickness is concerned, because it's more of a skill sport. And so I think certain positions—obviously pitching is one position where your legs are very important, but it's less critical, a different type of requirement, the same as catching. And with the designated hitter, you're going to see people rested at times, and so there's flexibility there.
But you just don't see old running backs, and you don't see Moses Malone playing thirty-five to forty minutes anymore. You don't see middle infielders continue to play the game at forty, where you have to have the quickness and the good first step.

Q: How about the mental side? Players say they run out of gas in their late thirties because they just don't have the desire anymore.
Ryan: I think their priorities change in life. It's hard to detect when that's going to happen. It's like anything

else, you have to learn to deal with it. There's a lot of times I'd rather be doing something else, but that's just the way it is.

I think it's the competitiveness in you, and that you prepare for whatever it is that you do. I think my approach would be the same if I were doing something else in some other field.

Q: Do you ever get tired of people asking you when you're going to retire?

Ryan: Well, I think it's an obvious question. I don't have an answer to that. Each year we get closer to it.

YOUR BODY AT 40

Okay, here comes the bad news. The inescapable, irre-versible truth: if you are 40 or more years old, you are on the downhill slide, physiologically speaking. You can-not escape the toll of time, try as you might to postpone it. You can only cope the best you can, treat the changes as the wages of experience, and take comfort in the fact that you certainly have a lot of company.

Scientists now estimate that the human body is de-signed to last for approximately 40 years. "After that, you're living on borrowed time," explains one anthro-pologist. "Your bones wear out, your teeth drop out, your digestion goes. After your peak reproductive years, Mother Nature doesn't care about you any more."

Allowing for individual variations—which certainly can be substantial—your body will probably be shorter and heavier at 40 than it was at 20. As the weight of gravity weakens your muscles, the disks between the bones of your spine deteriorate, causing you to lose perhaps a quarter inch of height per decade after the age of 30. And because you are probably less active at the same time that your metabolism is slowing by approximately 3 percent every decade, you will be burning less food; hence the average American male weighs 17 pounds more at the age of 40 than at 20. Worst of all, you may develop a chronic case of Dunlap's disease (as in, "Uh-oh, my stomach dunlapped over my belt").

Although body strength may peak in the late 30s and early 40s (assuming the body has been maintained in peak condition), endurance generally begins to deteriorate in the early 30s at a rate of about 1 percent per year; there appears to be nothing you can do about it. When you turn 40, your immune system begins to falter. Your sweat glands start to dry up. The lenses of your eyes become less pliable (a condition known as presbyopia), making it harder to focus on close objects and more difficult to scan a page quickly; however, this may also have the effect of correcting already existing cases of nearsightedness. Smile lines and crow's feet—from all that squinting you did when you were younger—begin to crease your face. In fact, your face will start to reflect whatever sort of expression you habitually put on it.

For the most part, a man's skin remains naturally younger looking longer than a woman's because of its higher oil content; the youngest-looking part of a man's skin at 40, though, is located rather uselessly on his buttocks, which (absent any exhibitionist inclinations) typically have been shielded from the aging effects of the sun's ultraviolet rays. At 40 a man's nose is wider and longer than it was at 30 due to the accumulation of cartilage. His ears and earlobes are longer and fatter, and his skull is thicker, the latter phenomenon being completely unrelated to the fact that he will probably score less well on memory and I.Q. tests than he did at 20.

Women's bodies, too, will contain a larger percentage of body fat after 40; in fact, women naturally become more fatty than men with age, though strenuous exercise can certainly slow the rate of increase. Whatever new fat accumulates will lodge mostly in her hips, thighs, and buttocks. Her chest size will grow, her pelvis widen, her breasts will droop—the inevitable effect of gravity—and her shoulders will narrow. Horizontal sleep lines may appear along the side of her chin.

By age 45, the average person's maximum heart rate is 94 percent of what it was at age 25; lung capacity is down to 82 percent; kidney function is 88 percent. Your sense of smell has started to become less keen; the breakdown of cells in the inner ear has robbed you of the ability to hear certain high-pitched noises, although you will still be able to hear every word your mate says. Permanent hair loss is a problem for nearly half of American men by their mid-40s. (It is small consolation that the hair in their ears, nostrils, and eyebrows tends to grow thicker and more rapidly at this age.) A woman's hair will simply start to grow thinner, and continue to do so for the rest of her life.

"Forty years on, growing older and older,
　　Shorter in wind, as in memory long,
　Feeble of foot, and rheumatic of shoulder,
　　What will it help you that once you were strong?"
　　　　　　　　　　　　　　—HARROW FOOTBALL SONG

"Middle age is the time when a man is always thinking that in a week or two he will feel as good as ever."
　　　　　　　　　　　　　　—DON MARQUIS

"An astonishing thing happened. As I got older, I got better-looking. Which is the reverse of what happens to most people. And by the time I was in my late 30s, I was starring in a movie."
　　　　　　　　　　　　　　—PAUL SIMON

Cathy ® is syndicated internationally by Universal Press Syndicate. Copyright © 1990 by Universal Press Syndicate.

"I spent so much of my youth wanting to look striking or beautiful that it was years before I realized that I was not exactly average looking, and not exactly ugly. I know now, approaching 40 myself, that the way a person looks is not really at all important." —PETE TOWNSEND

"Aside from a pair of noisy knees, I had never felt or looked better. Oh, there were a few tiny signs of age. The brown hair that used to tumble over my forehead now tumbles all the way to the floor. And of course, there's the pitter patter of little crow's feet around my eyes. But I'm lucky they're little; some crows have bigger feet than others." —JACK BENNY

"As tenors grow older, there is a natural tendency for the voice to darken, to grow darker like a baritone's vocal quality. . . . This development generally occurs around the age of forty. So I waited until I was forty before taking on Manrico, the bravura tenor role in Verdi's *Il Trovatore*." —LUCIANO PAVAROTTI

"The human primate becomes more interesting as his beauty fades. An old baboon is simply an ugly baboon, but a woman of 40 should have earned her crow's feet. Distrust, my children, the elderly unmarred face and remember that beauty is lavished on those who have nothing else to offer." —PETER S. PRESCOTT

"When I was thirty, thirty-five, forty, I sometimes looked in the mirror and quite liked what I saw. But it has never been the obsession for me that it is for some women to whom looks are everything, and who have a lot of difficulty coming to terms with growing old. To me the most important thing was my mind; everything else took second place." —SIMONE DE BEAUVOIR

"It may be true that life begins at forty, but everything else starts to wear out, fall out, or spread out."

—Beryl Pfizer

"After a woman passes her fortieth birthday she remains young as the result of constant precaution. Youth is no longer a matter of course."   —*Ladies Home Journal*, 1923

"A noisy forum of body parts takes the stand. Joints, muscles, and lower-back submit a petition, in creaks and aches, advising you to listen up. Facts are that the warranty on you ran out about three years ago, parts are irreplaceable, and mechanics cost about $3,000 an hour. It's time to 'racewalk' instead of jog. To work longer and harder to shed the excess weight. . . . No longer can you bound out of bed after a hard night's partying, eat a burrito, and face the world with exuberance and purpose."

—Joan Frank

"I think that everyone feels thirteen; everyone is surprised when the skin starts to get weird and the hair starts to fall out."

—Bette Midler

"I have everything I had twenty years ago, only it's all a little bit lower."

—Gypsy Rose Lee

"A woman of thirty-nine, a woman of a certain age! . . . I lift up my hair and see white streaks which are no longer just a curiosity or a trace but the beginning: soon my head will acquire while I am still alive the color of my bones. The complexion of my face might still seem supple and fresh but from one moment to the next the mask is going to slip, baring the rheumy eyes of an old woman. The seasons keep refurbishing themselves, defeats and dis-

asters can be repaired, but nothing can prevent my own decrepitude." —SIMONE DE BEAUVOIR,
IN *Les Mandarins*

"This middle-life thing has become a phobia; people think it's got to be a big problem, when it's simply not. I know from real life that middle-aged people are very attractive. I feel I'm beating out all those guys who stay on rigid diets. They run; they go crazy; their skin is always in fabulous shape. I feel like I'm going to scoop the pot going the other way." —JACK NICHOLSON

FITNESS AND BEAUTY TIPS FOR THOSE TURNING 40

In their neverending quest for immortality, Taoist monks in ancient China altered their diet according to the seasons, to keep their bodies in tune with nature. In winter, they instructed their disciples to eat Yang foods: meat (especially sausage), grains, eggs, and other foods that help to heat the body. Conversely, they believed that on hot summer nights one should consume only Yin foods: raw fish, juicy fruits, and cold vegetables.

Living in South Africa at the age of 40, Mohandas K. Gandhi often walked to and from his village home to the capital of Johannesburg, 21 miles away, in a single day. Arising at 2:00 A.M., Gandhi ate breakfast along the way, then had dinner upon his return at 5:30 in the afternoon before retiring early in the evening. His diet consisted largely of raw bananas, lemons, peanuts, oranges, and olive oil; he avoided all cooked foods entirely.

During his 40s, George Hamilton reportedly subsisted upon a diet rich in fruits, vegetables, and herbs, supplemented with protein powders, zinc, and heavy doses of megavitamins, with virtually no sweets, caffeine, or dairy products. During his occasional fasts, Hamilton maintained his blood-sugar level by drinking a mixture of eight ounces of cold water, the juice of two or three lemons, a dash of maple syrup, and half a teaspoon of cayenne pepper. Hamilton also allegedly journeyed to Switzerland for injections of fetal sheep cells in an attempt to rejuvenate his internal organs. And he insisted that each movie contract include a provision that his employers fly him to some beach spot so he could work on his tan. "I'll go anywhere for sun," declared Hamilton, "—North Africa, if necessary."

"Of course women forty years or more old have been told before this to relax completely for at least an hour in the middle of the day. This is undeniably good advice for the woman who can follow it." —*Ladies Home Journal*, 1923

"In middle age it is important and gratifying to be as handsome as possible, and certainly no one should be willing to be ugly or monstrous without putting up a battle. But the matter of diet should be a quiet, ascetic, personal business, just one more habit of living. It should not be the controlling force of a life, and it would not be if other ideals were not all out of whack."
—*Harper's Bazaar*, 1933

"Get ready for middle age in youth. Get ready for old age in your forties. And have your dentist x-ray those teeth. There's nothing like bad teeth in the forties to cause rheumatism in the fifties." —*Good Housekeeping*, 1938

"Don't give up meat. Don't cut out salt. Don't eat the same thing morning, noon, and night. Variety is everything—everything you need, everything in balance. Eating lots of different foods is what does your health and looks the greatest good."

> —*Harper's Bazaar "Diet to Save Your*
> *Health and Looks from 40 On,* 1975

"Avoid fried meats which angry up the blood."

> —SATCHEL PAIGE

"I eat all the time—anything and everything, in unbelievable amounts. It's funny—I was always very disciplined through my 20s and 30s, and now . . . I'm ready to party when everybody's decided to become disciplined."
> —FARRAH FAWCETT

"I staunchly believe that everything that can help a woman psychologically to overcome the trauma of aging is well worth the effort."
> —SOPHIA LOREN

"Do not try to live forever. You will not succeed."
> —GEORGE BERNARD SHAW

"Stay fit and think tough."
> —GEORGE BLANDA

"I do back-breaking exercise for an hour and a half every morning. . . . And, oh yes, eat a lot of grapefruit. I can't stand clothes that are tight, because they block off my psychic energy."
> —SHIRLEY MacLAINE

"I believe every woman, especially those over forty, needs the rejuvenation that a few moments alone can provide."
> —SOPHIA LOREN

"Know that 40 is beautiful—only now it just takes a little longer."
> —WAY BANDY

For your 40th birthday here's TWINKLES the BIRTHDAY FAIRY!! she can frolic and dance and leap around the room!

That's because Twinkles isn't 40 years old!

Happy Birthday!

Reprinted with permission from Hallmark Cards, Inc.

"Dear Diary: Can I look like Catherine Deneuve at forty-one?"

"Dear Writer: Did you look like Catherine Deneuve at twenty?"   —ELLEN GOODMAN

"Apply blusher sparingly; too much color looks particularly artificial on older women."   —*Woman's Day*, 1991

"As I get older, I've found the less I put on my face the better I look."   —BARBARA HOWAR

"It also helps to shave off your mustache, if you have one."   —PAUL SIMON

LOVE AND SEX AT
40

There's an old joke that goes, "What do you call a forty-year-old on a hot date?" "A chaperone." That's an easy laugh, but as you can tell from the "In Search of" columns of any local newspaper, the flame still burns bright for those on the far side of 40.

Especially for women. Simone Signoret once complained that our society allowed men to age gracefully, growing more distinguished (as did her husband, Yves Montand), while women simply got older. If this is true, Nature certainly evened up the score when it came to sex. Women over 40 can look forward to a far brighter future—though not necessarily with 40-year-old men.

Historical precedents abound. Catherine the Great, the eighteenth-century empress of Russia who built a well-deserved historical reputation for her voracious sexual appetite, did not take her first lover until after she was 46 years old. Then she did not waste her time with men her own age, but chose much younger lovers instead. "Men make love more intensely at twenty," she decided, "but make love better, however, at thirty." Casanova, on the other hand, was pretty much washed up by the time he hit 40.

Ever since Masters and Johnson completed their landmark study of human sexuality, it has become increasingly evident that the average woman's sexual responsiveness peaks in her late 30s and remains at or near that level until well into her 60s. Her physical changes during arousal vary remarkably little from the time she was 20, while the inhibitions and self-doubts that may earlier have hindered her pleasure have vanished with years of experience.

Of course, sexual therapists insist that statistical surveys may mask a wide range of "normal" behavior, and that one should not worry if one does not fit into whatever category passes for average. What is most important, they say, is the entire relationship between two individuals, rather than the purely physical aspects of sex.

Nevertheless, there can be little doubt that for men the news is not so good, though the outlook is not nearly as bleak as Dr. Alfred Kinsey made it appear when he reported several decades ago that men are in a continuous state of sexual decline after reaching their peak at the age of 17. According to Dr. Alex Comfort, the primary changes that an average healthy 40-year-old male may expect are that he will be "less easily able to respond with a quick erection to purely visual stimuli, like the mere sight of a woman, and that he less easily gets an orgasm with every act of intercourse." Hence the appearance of advertisements such as:

YOU MEN PAST 40 TRY THIS!

All in? Lack Vigor? Have you lost your
Courage and Grow Tired too soon?

or

EXERCISE YOUR TROUBLE SPOTS!

At the age of 40, the typical male will have 84 orgasms per year (8 solo), compared to his previous high of 121 orgasms at the age of 30. But if such intimations of mortality cause a small percentage of men to seek out younger women to rejuvenate their psyches (particularly if their sense of self-worth is vitally connected to their sexual performance), behaviorists tend to agree that most men accept these changes pretty calmly. Chances are that most 40-year-old males have already discovered other interests to fill their evenings—and besides, they're much too tired anyway.

"When you buy an automobile, they give you a wonderful book that tells how to turn the key and what to do if something goes wrong. Most people find out about sex through on-the-job training. They start at fourteen or fifteen and make mistakes for thirty years. By the time they really get the hang of it, it's too late."

—Dr. David R. Reuben

"Instead of telling kids very early about the mechanics and nothingness of sex, maybe it would be better to suddenly and very excitingly reveal the details to them when they're forty. You could be walking down the street with a friend who's just turned forty, spill the birds-and-the-bees beans, wait for the initial shock of learning what-goes-where to die down, and then patiently explain the rest. Then suddenly at forty their life would have new meaning. We should really stay babies for much longer than we do, now that we're living much longer."

—Andy Warhol

"The advice from all sides is: you need all the sex you can get. Regular sexual relations are an absolute must to keep the body in good working order. Imagine being told to put sex ahead of brushing your teeth. Well, there you are—up and at it. It's important, because any part of your body that is not used constantly for the next 40 years will just wither away."

—JANE OGLE, in "Sex Begins at Forty"

"At the age of forty [a woman] is very far from being cold and insensible; her fire may be covered with ashes, but it is not extinguished."

—LADY MARY WORTLEY MONTAGU

"An absolutely wonderful sexual ripening occurs at 40. . . . As I crept up on that 40th birthday, a slow awakening began to take place. By some standards, maybe I wasn't young anymore, but my libido certainly didn't know that. . . . Sex at 40 has a languorous quality and is so much more sensual. Practice doesn't necessarily make perfect, but it certainly enhances the pleasure." —JANET DAILEY

"I'm here to say that we will get the jobs we want when we are past 40, and that we will have sex until we die. Life doesn't end when your flip blond hairdo is cut off."

—SALLY JESSY RAPHAEL

"Sexuality is really more important after forty—and making love makes a woman look terrific." —RITA MORENO

"I am forty-two. It's not so bad; I should be able to pick up somebody." —JOAN BAEZ

"The mature woman has awakened to the fact that she is neither a shrinking violet nor a century plant. She is more like an exotic bloom—difficult to cultivate, vaguely mysterious, exotically beautiful and surprisingly sturdy. . . . She no longer feels a need to apologize for her age, abdicate her allure and stifle the sexual desires which do

not automatically disappear with the lighting of the fortieth or fiftieth candle on her birthday cake."

—HELEN VAN SLYKE

"The increased awareness of sexuality and the woman's
right to orgasm is very depressing to men. You take a 45-
year-old woman who's never had an orgasm. He isn't
about to deal with that at his age."

—NORMAN SHERESKY

In November 1951, dramatist Laurence S. Liebson, age
51, asked a New York court to grant him a divorce from
his wife of 9 months. His new bride, he claimed, had
deceived him, during their half-year courtship, by pretending to be "a maiden of 26." After their wedding,
however, Liebson had discovered to his surprise that he
had married a woman who was actually 48 years old and
a grandmother of two. In her defense, Doraine Liebson
introduced her physical charms as her primary exhibits:
"My pulchritude exceeds my mental endowment, which
exceeds that of my bookish husband," she sniffed. "In
truth, I could keep a husband so happy, give him inex-
haustible pleasures and could bubble over with the right
man because I am many women all rolled into one."
Impressed with Mrs. Liebson's spunk and, perhaps, her
legs as well, the judge ordered her estranged husband to
pay Doraine's legal fees and $125 weekly alimony.

"At twenty, if a girl gives you a long, direct look and
smiles, you look into the next weighing-machine mirror
to see why you are so attractive. At forty you look to see
who's behind you or what's unbuttoned."

—ROBERT M. YODER

"By the time I was twenty, the forty-year-olds seemed
romantic—they had a life behind them, they had a sharply

distinct personality; and I pondered about the somewhat battered but deeply experienced woman that I should be one day. But it seemed to me entirely out of place that people of such an age should presume to have affairs or even to flirt. I was at a party at the Atelier when I was twenty-five, and I looked at all the 'well-preserved' creatures there, thinking of them as so many old hags. Even when I was thirty-five it shocked me when I heard older people referring to the amorous side of their married life; there comes a time, thought I, when one should in decency give up that sort of thing."

—SIMONE DE BEAUVOIR

"It does change the age that is young, once in Paris it was twenty-six, then it was twenty-two, then it was nineteen and now it is between thirty and forty."

—GERTRUDE STEIN

Fiction is stranger than fact. In Grace Metallious's novel *Return to Peyton Place*, middle-aged literary agent Bradley Holmes became the object of young Allison MacKenzie's overheated affections. (Anyone with a working knowledge of middle-aged literary agents will realize just how preposterous a notion this really is.) Described by Metallious as "forty years old, dark haired, and powerfully built," Holmes soon found himself overwhelmed by his virgin admirer, and soon the two were enjoying an illicit weekend tryst in a rocky valley in rural Connecticut.

Vladimir Nabokov's *Lolita*, of course, deals with the same subject, but from the opposite perspective. Humbert Humbert, the narrator and pursuer of his adored nymphet Lolita (actually, the girl is barely 12 when the book opens), ages from 37 to 42 over the course of the story; by the end, his somewhat unorthodox obsession has made him a broken man and driven him to attempt murder.

"Forty-five is a difficult age in monogamous societies, because many men and women approach it with the fear of having missed their youth and proceed with reckless speed to try to catch up with it." —AURO ROSELLI

"I've arrived at the age [40] when boy flappers are supposed to appeal to me, but they don't. They bore me to death with their limpid eyes and their sex talk." —EDNA FERBER

"A man is at his best between 36 and 60. No question. That's when he takes over, is assured of himself. But a woman? I have to tell you, nobody ever asked Eleanor Roosevelt to dance. Oh, we all loved the way she looked. But no one said, 'There's a dishy number over there.' Nobody said, 'Let's mambo!' " —JOAN RIVERS

In July 1986, the bikini celebrated its 40th birthday. When French designer Louis Réard first unveiled his creation—three patches of cotton (129 square inches in all) covered with a newsprint pattern and held together by a pair of flimsy strings—in Paris during the first year after World War II, all the local models refused to wear it in public. Finally, Réard had to hire a stripper to show it off. Spurred by the prelates of the Catholic Church, the governments of Italy, Spain, Belgium, and Portugal banned bikinis from their beaches. Reaction in the United States was only slightly less hysterical; even in relatively sophisticated sections of the country, women brazen enough to wear bikinis on the beach were routinely removed and charged with indecent exposure. Not until Brigitte Bardot appeared at the Cannes Film Festival clad in a bikini did the brief two-piece suit achieve at least a measure of acceptance, if not respectability.

"At eighteen, one adores at once; at twenty, one loves; at thirty, one desires; at forty, one reflects."

—PAUL DE KOCK

"Be in love for the first time at forty? I think that if a woman hasn't loved before forty, if she hasn't had a great love before forty, she will never have it."

—MELINA MERCOURI

♦ ♦ ♦ ♦

"A bachelor who has passed forty is a remnant; there is no good material in him." —HELEN ROWLAND

"If you're still not married by the time you're 25, they're worried about you. By the time you're 30, they give up on you. By the time you're 45, they're sitting shiva [in mourning]." —JACKIE MASON

Bachelors at Forty

Warren Beatty
Voltaire
George Bernard Shaw
Ludwig Van Beethoven
Plato
President James Buchanan
Jackie Mason
Tom Wolfe
Edward, Prince of Wales
(the future Edward VIII
of England)

Isaac Newton
Adolf Hitler
Justice David Souter
Mick Jagger
George Hamilton
Charles Baudelaire
Grover Cleveland
Martin Luther

And an estimated three million American men

◆ ◆ ◆ ◆

"There's a magic about numbers. Thirty, forty, fifty
. . . it's been imposed by the culture. All those rules about
who you can love and who you can't love and how.
. . . Why should I deprive myself of my adventure, which
is my life, of going through something for the first time
because perhaps I am not twenty any more? Why should
I defer to society in that way?"   —JEANNE MOREAU

"I'm forty and no woman can know what falling in love
can mean until she's forty."   —MARIE LLOYD

"Finally, finally, I am loved! This is it, I know this is it!
For the very first time in my life I'm happy, really happy!
I have never been so happy!"
                              —JUDY GARLAND, at 47,
                    after marrying for the fifth time

One of the greatest love stories of all time was the
romance between Elizabeth Barrett and Robert Browning.
A rather plain woman to begin with, Barrett was an in-
valid spinster whose medication had turned her into a
morphine addict afraid to leave the confines of her tiny
room in Wimpole Street—she had not been outside in 5
years—when she fell in love with Browning, 6 years her
junior. Because of Elizabeth's infirmity and her father's
disapproval of Browning, the couple carried on their affair
by correspondence until, shortly after her 40th birthday,
Elizabeth began to reestablish contact with the outside
world. Six months later they were married secretly and,
fearing the wrath of Elizabeth's father, ran away for a
honeymoon in Italy.

"At the age of forty, men that love love rootedly. If the love is plucked from them, the life goes with it."
—GEORGE MEREDITH

"For real true love, love at first sight, love to devotion, love that robs a man of his sleep, love that 'will gaze an eagle blind,' love that 'will hear the lowest sound when the suspicious tread of theft is stopped,' love that is 'like a Hercules, still climbing trees in the Hesperides,'—we believe the best age is from forty-five to seventy; up to that, men are generally given to mere flirting."
—ANTHONY TROLLOPE

Probably no affair did more to enhance the public image of 40-year-old women than the celebrated romance between King Edward VIII of England and Wallis Warfield Simpson. Despite a wealth of criticism in the press of their personal shortcomings, the vision of a king forsaking his throne for the love of a 40-year-old woman—Mrs. Simpson celebrated her birthday just 6 months before Edward abdicated—gave the age of 40 a luster and allure it really had never enjoyed before.

SEX SYMBOLS AT 40 (OR SOMETHING)

Turning 40 can be an especially traumatic experience for entertainers whose success depends primarily upon their physical appearance. Elizabeth Taylor once recounted a story that her friend Sidney Guilaroff, Hollywood hairstylist to the stars, had told her about Marilyn Monroe: "Sidney said that she was terrified of turning forty. 'She came to get her hair done one day,' he told me, 'and while I was combing her out, she leaned forward into the mirror, put her hands to her face, and cried, 'Oh, God, Sidney, look at these wrinkles. Oh God, Sidney, am I getting old?' "

Three days later Marilyn was dead, at the age of 36.

Greta Garbo, too, seemed unable to cope with the prospect of turning 40. Elsa Maxwell once spied the reclusive star gazing at herself in a powder-room mirror at a Hollywood party. "Garbo was staring so intently into the mirror that she did not hear me enter," recalled Maxwell. "I have no idea how long she had been studying her reflection, but she shuddered suddenly and buried her head in her arms. Only she could have found a flaw in that exquisite face. Only a woman with a morbid fear of age could have failed to see that time would enhance the beauty of her classic features and magnificent bone structure. She was 35 and all she could see were middle-aged roles in her future. Then, as now, she would not mature gracefully—and she never will."

And yet other sex symbols turn 40 with barely a rueful glance backward; some have managed to hang onto their beauty for a few years more, while others are simply relieved to no longer have to keep up appearances.

♦ ♦ ♦ ♦

"I am a phenomenon."
  —BRIGITTE BARDOT, 40, after posing for nude
     photographs that appeared in *Playboy* magazine

"I'm a good example of what a forty-year old woman should look like. I am remarkably healthy and I have a good—no, a great body. So it would be silly for me to hide behind thirty-nine forever. Society places an accent on youth, but the bloom is still on this rose."
  —VICTORIA PRINCIPAL, 40

"What I've really got a good take on is tits. Because I've had mine for so long, and they're such a big part of me. I weigh more now than I've ever weighed, more than I could ever conceive of someone my size weighing. But you know what? I was zooming in toward forty, and I suddenly realized I didn't care anymore how I looked. It's a great weight off my mind."   —BETTE MIDLER, 40

"I'm becoming more attractive with age. I'm getting to look less like a punk. I want to be leading-man age. I think I'll be gorgeous at 50."   —WOODY ALLEN, 40

"I was terrified when I turned 30. I was pregnant and had the mumps. . . . But strangely enough, as I turn 40, my gray hairs and wrinkles don't bother me very much. I think it's because I'm happy. That always helps. And it's because I'm discovering that if you work at it and if you're lucky, you really can get wiser. I wouldn't want to go back."
                                                    —JANE FONDA, 40

"The realization hit me that here I was forty years old— I looked pretty good, I thought I was really a good actress, better than people had given me credit for—and they always noticed my looks more than what I was doing, and I wanted to have it again, have the career. So . . . I appeared all over England playing a very sexy role, taking off all my clothes in an X-rated film. It started my career again."
                                                    —JOAN COLLINS

"If I could age like my mother, I'd be very, very happy, but I doubt whether I will grow old gracefully."
                                                    —ELIZABETH TAYLOR, 40

"As anyone who's used looks as a crutch for attaining fame and fortune, I have trepidation about the aging process, but I truly believe I'm entering a better, more so- phisticated stage of my life. I'm at the apex of my prime."
                                                    —RAQUEL WELCH, nearing 40

"As far as I can tell, not one of the new breed of midlife beauties is going to make their peers feel good about themselves. It's Rosemary Clooney in a muumuu who makes them feel good. What Loren, Fonda, Welch, etc., have done is to raise the threshold of self-hate faster than the age span.

"We no longer look forward to letting go at thirty. There is no thought of aging gracefully at forty. At fifty, we are faced with a prospect of daily regimens to soften our skin and tighten our thighs. The end result of all this is that those of us who failed to look like Brooke Shields at seventeen can now fail to look like Victoria Principal at thirty-three and like Linda Evans at forty-one . . ."

—ELLEN GOODMAN

"A fellow grabbed hold of me today, a dignified guy, and told me he'd been a fan of mine when he was just an office boy or something in the dress business. Well, let's face it. I'm forty, and the kids I used to sing for are getting up there, too."   —FRANK SINATRA, 40

"It used to be underwear and hotel keys [that fans threw onstage]. Now I get flowers."   —TOM JONES, 40

"It seemed to me that I had grown old. I found enjoyment of love less vivid, less seductive, and my vitality had greatly diminished. Besides, I found that I no longer interested the fair sex at first sight and that certain women preferred my rivals to myself."   —CASANOVA

"I look like a discouraged beetle battered by the rains of a spring night. I look like a molting bird. I look like a governess in distress. I look—Good L—d, I look like an actress on tour, and that speaks for itself."

—COLETTE, 40

"I don't think of myself in terms of age. I know I'm aging, but I'm not going to destroy the years I have left worrying about it."   —JEANNE MOREAU, after 40

"People come up to me, perfect strangers, and ask me to take off my dark glasses so they can have a look at my eyes. My answer is simple. I just say, 'Is that all you think of me?' Are they going to write on my tombstone, 'Here lies Paul Newman who died a failure at the age of 43 because his eyes turned brown'? If blue eyes are what it's all about, and not the accumulation of my work as a professional actor, I may as well turn in my union card right now and go into gardening." —PAUL NEWMAN, 40

"I heard Jacqueline Bisset is 40. Maybe I can meet her now."
—REGGIE JACKSON, 40

"You go into these strange rooms and you can feel yourself being examined. It's like, 'There she is. What do you think now? How is she holding up?' . . . I know, with my name and face, I carry a certain baggage into whatever I do. I'll never be able to get away from that completely. But here I am, in my 40s. At some point, they all have to face up to the fact that I've changed, that we all change."
—FARRAH FAWCETT, 42

"Age is how you feel about yourself. I particularly like what a Frenchman once said to me on the subject: 'From thirty-five to forty-five women are old. Then the devil takes over certain women at forty-five and they become beautiful, mature, warm—in a word, splendid. The acidities are gone, and in their place reigns calm. Such women are worth going out to find because the men who find them never grow old.' "
—SOPHIA LOREN, 44

"My forties are the best time I have ever gone through."
—ELIZABETH TAYLOR, after 40

"It's funny: when I was twenty I looked younger than I was. Now, at forty, I look older than I am. God, I'll only be able to play old parts now!" —LAURENCE OLIVIER, 40

"In the brain, age is like a good wine—it gets better. But age below the brain isn't like wine at all—it gets worse down there."
—JULIO IGLESIAS, 47

"What I really hate is watching Robert Redford get younger and younger leading ladies. We're living in a society that makes it more difficult for women to get older than men. There is a definite double standard. . . . Traditionally the big women stars hit forty or forty-five and vanish—just disappear. Then, years later, they resurface as big character stars and have a whole new career. . . .

"Sure I wish I was forty again, but I'm not, so why waste time moaning about it?"   —JANE FONDA, 47

"It's the decomposition that gets me. You spent your whole life looking after your body. And then you rot away."   —BRIGITTE BARDOT, 47

WHERE WERE THEY
AT
40?

If you have reached 40 and still have not made your first million or written the Great American Novel, do not despair. (I haven't, and I don't. All right, maybe I do get a little depressed sometimes.) Instead, take a look at the following list of famous historical personalities—from gangsters to financiers, from Wild West desperadoes to world conquerors—to see where they were at 40. Some of them, of course, had not yet achieved anything of consequence, while others were either dead or already burned out.

And for those of you who are feeling pretty smug about having reached the top of the ladder before turning 40, just remember that Napoleon and Donald Trump probably were congratulating themselves at the same age. So there.

Billy the Kid—Dead at the age of 21.
Napoleon Bonaparte—His empire stood at its zenith, en-

compassing virtually all of Western Europe (save Britain, of course)—nearly 70 million people. But Napoleon never won another significant military victory after his 40th birthday.

Lenny Bruce—Dead of a heroin overdose at the age of 40, after wasting the last two years of his life fighting petty obscenity and narcotics prosecutions.

Al Capone—Incarcerated at Terminal Island, San Pedro, California, serving the last months of an 11-year sentence for tax evasion and contempt.

Stokely Carmichael—Living in Guinea and serving as a "revolutionary apprentice" to brutal dictator Sékou Touré.

Kit Carson—Retired from frontier scouting business at 39. Trying to make a living as a rancher in what is now New Mexico.

Butch Cassidy (Robert Leroy Parker)—Living in South America (first Argentina, then Bolivia), hiding from the law, and robbing banks and payrolls.

George Armstrong Custer—Dead at the age of 36. (Well, it was pretty much his own fault.)

John Dillinger—Dead at the age of 31.

Bob Dylan—A born-again Christian whose albums were going nowhere.

Henry Ford—Barely had his financial head above water. After building experimental racing and passenger cars, he founded the Ford Motor Company six weeks before he turned 40.

Geronimo—An Apache warrior, living peacefully in New Mexico.

Abbie Hoffman—On the run, living underground after jumping bail while facing a lengthy jail sentence for dealing cocaine.

John Henry "Doc" Holliday—Dead at the age of 36.

Jack Kerouac—An overweight alcoholic, drinking a quart of cognac a day, barely able to pronounce his own name, and wholly out of touch with reality.

Chinggis (Genghis) Khan—Still known by his given name, Temujin; just one of several Mongol tribal chieftains. Became the Great Khan at age 44, then embarked on his initial military campaigns in China.

Meyer Lansky—Living quietly in Omaha, Nebraska, pondering an investment in the dog racing business.

John Lennon—A self-described "househusband," Lennon recorded his first album in 5 years (*Double Fantasy*) shortly before his 40th birthday. Three weeks after he turned 40, Lennon was dead, murdered by a psychotic fan on the street in front of his apartment.

Abraham Lincoln—Apparently washed up as a political figure, having lost his reelection bid after only one term in Congress. Turning his back on politics, Lincoln returned to Springfield, Illinois, to resume his law practice.

Harry Longbaugh ("The Sundance Kid")—Living in South America with Cassidy.

Lucky Luciano—Incarcerated at Dannemora penitentiary in upstate New York, serving a 30-to-50-year sentence for prostitution racketeering.

Michael Milken—Earning approximately $550.1 million in direct compensation from Drexel Burnham Lambert, the highest annual paycheck in U.S. corporate history.

George "Baby Face" Nelson—Dead at the age of 26.

Florence Nightingale—Perhaps the second most famous woman in Britain, following her campaign for medical reform during the Crimean War.

Richard Milhous Nixon—Celebrated his 40th birthday two weeks before his inauguration as the second-youngest Vice President in U.S. history.

Ronald Reagan—An actor in Hollywood, making *Bedtime for Bonzo*.

John D. Rockefeller—One of the wealthiest men in America, after building Standard Oil into a virtual monopoly of the oil pipeline and refining business in the United States.

Franklin Delano Roosevelt—Recovering from poliomyelitis, suffered the previous year. In 1920, at the age of 38, Roosevelt had lost in a landslide as the Democratic nominee for Vice President.

Mayer Amschel Rothschild—A successful but hardly wealthy merchant in Frankfurt, dealing mainly in cloth, wine, and tobacco.

Jerry Rubin—An unabashed capitalist. After joining a Wall Street firm as a securities analyst, Rubin launched a chain of upscale Manhattan business networking salons.

Sylvester "Sly" Stone—Undergoing treatment at a mental clinic in Fort Myers, Florida, to kick a freebase habit.

Zachary Taylor—Serving as superintendent of recruiting for the Western Department of the U.S. Army. Apparently he was still in good health.

Harry Truman—A judge in Jackson County, Missouri. Truman was voted out of office midway through his 40th year and subsequently earned his living for a time by selling memberships in the Kansas City Automobile Club.

Donald Trump—Ruler of a real estate empire with an estimated worth of $2 billion. Holdings included the Trump Tower, the New Jersey Generals football team, the Grand Hyatt Hotel, and two Atlantic City casinos.

THE DREADED
MIDLIFE CRISIS

So much nonsense has been written on the subject of the midlife crisis that one is tempted to assume it is all just the figment of some pop psychologists' overheated imaginations. Certainly the notion has been used to justify all sorts of irrational and irresponsible behavior—just because you don't feel like going to work on a sunny spring morning doesn't mean you're having a midlife crisis—and it may be only a matter of time before some particularly creative trial attorney tries to employ it as a defense for his or her client.

But if our culture does place too much emphasis upon the mere fact of turning 40 as a dividing point in life (and of course it does), this exaggeration, like many others, has its origin in a fundamental and significant truth about the human condition. At the age of 40, we are literally at the midpoint of our lives, and the onset of a psychological crisis at this age is a very real phenomenon.

"At any kind of significant turning point or life passage," notes Dr. Susan Blumenthal, chief of the behavioral medicine research program at the National Institute of Mental Health, "there is an assessment of what one has accomplished, and what is left to do. Oftentimes there is a preoccupation with a sense of mortality. At forty, one's parents are older or are dying, at forty there is an awareness of one's own finitude. And if there are children in the teenage years, sometimes there is an assessment of the old age behind you, and the youth ahead of you." For men, the crisis may be intensified by fears of a loss of virility.

Although the terminology may be of recent origin, the concept of a midlife crisis is hardly a novel one. As you will note from the examples below, history is full of 40-year-old men and women running off with younger partners in an attempt to regain the illusion of youth. At the age of 43, Paul Gauguin, the late nineteenth-century French Postimpressionist painter, left behind his business in Paris and ran off to paint and procreate in Tahiti. And shortly after Leo Tolstoy turned 40, the Russian novelist completed his final revisions to *War and Peace*, one of the greatest works in the history of prose fiction, and walked right into an attack of extreme anxiety because he felt he had already reached the pinnacle of his career. What more could he do with his life? "It was two o'clock in the morning," Tolstoy wrote to a friend after he had recovered his nerve. "I was terribly tired, I wanted to go to sleep and I felt perfectly well. But suddenly I was overcome by despair, fear and terror, the like of which I have never experienced before. . . . Life and death somehow merged into one another."

So what advice can we offer? "Now is the time to stop running, to slow down and reflect, to start developing your own depths," suggests psychologist Dr. Martin Symonds. "Now is the time to examine yourself—your feelings, your wants, your possibilities—so that you can live with yourself as you are, with no deception, no fraud, no 'buts.' In other words, you accept yourself respectfully."

◆ ◆ ◆ ◆

"They say the forties are the dangerous ages."
—HOWARD MUMFORD JONES

"Forty's kind of like New Year's. It's an age to think about what you've done up till now, and what you ought to do in the future."   —ERIC BERNE

"Forty—somber anniversary to the hedonist—in seekers after truth like Buddha, Mahomet, Mencius, St. Ignatius, the turning-point of their lives."   —CYRIL CONNOLLY

"When you get to be around forty, it's very necessary to make a break, or to effect some kind of wrench in your life. Suppose you start in a profession at the age of twenty-five, and make some progress in that field—after fifteen years it can become very repetitive and you should be able to call off all the answers pretty quickly. I find that I've been repeating myself in performances, and in judgments, because I've burned out creatively. I can't invent any more. I've done it."   —PAUL NEWMAN

"I completely lost my zest for everything. I went through my singing assignments with no enthusiasm. The applause no longer worked like a hypodermic on my system. Everything had lost its point. This was incredible for me. . . . The problem, I'm sure, had something to do with having finally arrived and wondering what I had arrived at. There comes a point when you feel trapped by your voice. It is not a matter of wishing you were doing something else, only that, because of the voice, you cannot do anything else."   —LUCIANO PAVAROTTI

Cathy ® is syndicated internationally by Universal Press Syndicate. Copyright © 1990 by Universal Press Syndicate.

"The world is divided into those who have mid-life crises and those who give them."   —*Esquire*, 1980

"From twenty to thirty, I was trying to learn how to act. From thirty to forty, I was enjoying the opportunity to work at will. From forty to—I'm in my midlife crisis. . . .

"I wake up screaming. When you're not successful, you strive to be successful. And after you're successful, you strive to stay successful. Suddenly I thought, Something's missing. There's an emptiness. I don't want to go from forty to fifty the way I went from thirty to forty."
                                                   —DUSTIN HOFFMAN

"It's certainly there, but it isn't a gnawing fear. When you pass forty, you know that time is running out. But it always has been for me. Ever since I was eighteen years old."   —SHIRLEY MacLAINE

"When I was soon to come upon the age of forty, a figure chosen arbitrarily to be half of the expected years of my life, I found myself being acutely aware of the quickened chirping of birds and the accelerated ticking of clocks and the speedy conclusion of thoughts and judgments unlike the deliberate pondering in the past. Time was trying to catch up with me. There was so much to do and so much desire for accomplishment that there was a constant urgency to eliminate this or to select that other thing in order for the best among the good to be chosen."
                                                   —ERSKINE CALDWELL

"When an unsuccessful man passes that magic number [forty] he reacts to frustration and unhappiness by eating himself out of shape. The successful man reacts to good fortune by becoming a glutton. Either way the body is the same, even if the tailoring is different."
                                                   —JOEY ADAMS

"It's that word 'middle.' Any phrase it touches becomes the label of the frump; middle of the road, middle class, middle age. If only you could leap these dreary decades and land up in the important numbers. There is chic to seventy, elegance to eighty. People ought to be one of two things, young or old. No; what's the good of fooling? People ought to be one of two things, young or dead."
—DOROTHY PARKER

"In all of the theories about why so many people have attacks of wackiness when they reach middle age—resign from the bank to go live in a van with a teen-age mushroom gatherer, and that sort of thing—one factor has been neglected: When someone reaches middle age, people he knows begin to get put in charge of things, and knowing what he knows about the people who are being put in charge of things scares the hell out of him. If he's one of the people put in charge of things himself, it may scare him all the more. In his heart of hearts, he knows how he made it through English 137, and he suspects others may know."
—CALVIN TRILLIN

"The slow discovery by a novelist of his individual method can be exciting, but a moment comes in middle age when he feels that he no longer controls his method; he has become its prisoner. Then a long period of ennui sets in; it seems to him he has done everything before."
—GRAHAM GREENE

"You develop a fussy and ill-tempered sensitivity toward the very presence of so many other people in the same city, even on the same continent. The young love crowds, tumult and touching in gangs. You luxuriate in fantasies of lonely cabins on mountain tops at the end of dirt roads, out-of-season hotels on forgotten islands cut off by stormy tides, hunting trips in trackless forests where the only unshootable living creature is the woodcutter's lovely daughter. You seek the empty car on the train, the isolated seat on the plane, the road along which all the automobiles are speeding in the opposite direction."

—ALAN BRIEN

"I was then very much in the middle of my life, enjoying great success, but I knew that it would not be sufficient. I had designed elegant and profitable collections of ladies' clothing. I would soon have enough money to last two lifetimes, but was that all there was to it? Would Oleg Cassini be just a woman's fashion designer?"

—OLEG CASSINI

"It's fear that makes us old. In a new career, you don't know what to be afraid of. You're young again, creative, alive."   —ERNEST K. GANN, who left his job as an airline pilot at 42 to write full-time

"At 40, you do start to think about things differently. I must say, I can understand why people eventually stop making pictures—because to make films in such an impassioned way, you really have to believe in it, you've really got to want to tell that story, and after a while, you may find out life itself is more important than the filmmaking process. Maybe the answer for what the hell we're doing here has to be in the process of living itself, rather than in the work."   —MARTIN SCORSESE

"And why is analysis impossible for most people over forty? Because they couldn't stand to look back on their lives without the impression of an enormous failure. You always have the impression you are losing something, but you are really not."   —JEANNE MOREAU

"If a man's curve of efficiency is ascending at 45, and keeps on ascending just after that period, it may well

move upward for his whole life; but if there is a turn downward at 45, he will never recover."
—NICHOLAS MURRAY BUTLER

"Many people never climb above the plateau of forty-to-fifty. The signs that presage growth, so similar, it seems to me, to those in early adolescence: discontent, restlessness, doubt, despair, longing, are interpreted falsely as signs of decay. . . . Instead of facing them, one runs away; one escapes—into depressions, nervous breakdowns, drink, love affairs, or frantic, thoughtless, fruitless overwork."
—ANNE MORROW LINDBERGH

"At sixteen I was stupid, confused, insecure and indecisive. At twenty-five I was wise, self-confident, prepossessing and assertive. At forty-five I am stupid, confused, insecure and indecisive. Who would have supposed that maturity is only a short break in adolescence?"
—JULES FEIFFER

"I feel threatened, vulnerable, limited by time—I want to complete my tree. . . . I want to become something other than myself, and quickly. I'm no longer interested in myself. My teeth, my liver, and the rest are moldering away and my body is of no intrinsic interest. I want to be something different when it is time to die."
—ANTOINE DE SAINT-EXUPÉRY

"Forty-five is the age of recklessness for many men, as if in defiance of the decay and death waiting with open arms in the sinister valley at the bottom of the inevitable hill. For every age is fed on illusions, lest men should renounce life early and the human race come to an end."
—JOSEPH CONRAD

"I'm at my midlife journey, that's for sure. I'm in a dark wood, babe. I feel often like a neophyte on the road. I really do. I don't say that immodestly. I still feel very innocent, in many ways."   —OLIVER STONE

"I think that at forty Larry [Olivier] had lost the basic need that propels every actor. And yet he knew that he could not just give up acting—it was a duty he felt he owed to the public. So thereafter he approached it more as a duty than an enthusiasm. . . . In this way he was a very mature man at forty—indeed, more mature than his years might have called for. But he had done so much, achieved so much, that his attitude toward life was almost world-weary, as though it was impossible for him to get any more thrills out of his life or career."
                    —HARCOURT WILLIAMS

"I know for a fact that in every state of this damned Union there are still attractive women in their early forties who want to chuck hubby and take off for more excitement in a bigger town. There's a desperation many women know in their early forties, when they're afraid life is passing them by."   —KING VIDOR

"Most over-40 men leave their wives for someone else. Women of that age seem to leave their husbands for something else."   —ELLEN GOODMAN

Divorces at 40

James Thurber was 40 when he divorced his wife and moved into a hotel room, where he took to throwing his soiled laundry into the closet instead of sending it to the cleaners. His wardrobe was rescued when he married his second wife within the year.

At 40, Frank Lloyd Wright left his wife and six children for another woman. He built his new lover a low, rambling, spacious house at Spring Green. Two years later, while Wright was out of town, a servant went berserk and killed Wright's mistress, burning down the house, too.

After he turned 40, Erskine Caldwell divorced his second wife, photographer Margaret Bourke-White, and subsequently married a 20-year-old University of Arizona coed.

Shortly after his 40th birthday, the emperor Napoleon divorced Josephine. He tried to blame the move on the imperative of public opinion: "All France desires a divorce and claims it loudly. I cannot oppose my country's will."

At 40, middle-aged playboy Philippe Junot decided to separate from Princess Caroline of Monaco; conductor André Previn left his wife, Dory, for Mia Farrow; and Anita Bryant divorced her husband. When Jane Russell was 40, she told her husband, former football star Bob Waterfield, that she wanted a divorce, though the split did not become official for another seven years.

♦ ♦ ♦ ♦

Most Times Married by 40

5—Tammy Wynette
   Elizabeth Taylor
   Enos "Country" Slaughter

4—Christina Onassis (by the time she was 33, in fact)
   Mickey Rooney
   Zsa Zsa Gabor
   Judy Garland

♦ ♦ ♦ ♦

"Actually, my midlife crisis is that I am not having a crisis. Like Napoleon pacing the deck of the Bellerophon, I pace my study, my forehead corrugated by concentration, wondering why I have been denied this crisis, this badge of seriousness, this excuse for going off the rails."

—GEORGE F. WILL

JERRY GREENFIELD

On March 14, 1990, Jerry Greenfield, co-founder of Ben and Jerry's Homemade Ice Cream, celebrated his 40th birthday. His partner, Ben Cohen, turned 40 just four days later. Long dedicated to the proposition that eating is one of the primary joys in life, Ben and Jerry commiserated together over the depressing fact that their 40-year-old stomachs could no longer hold as much food as in their younger days. Other than that, however, they both seemed to be holding up pretty well.

As any self-respecting ice cream gourmand knows, Ben and Jerry's likenesses may be found on the lids of their ice cream cartons; Jerry is the good-looking one without the beard and hat.

Q: When you were twenty, would you have guessed that you'd be doing what you're doing, now that you're forty?
Jerry: Absolutely not.

Q: What would you have guessed?

Jerry: At the time, I was in college, in a pre-med program, so I probably would have thought that I would be a doctor, or working for someone else. I never would have guessed that I would have started a company with someone else, charting my own path as opposed to just plugging into a system.

Q: I understand. I just turned forty myself last year, and—

Jerry: How was it?

Q: Fine, until I started doing the research for this book. But how did you and Ben get into this business?

Jerry: Well, Ben and I are old friends from junior high school, so we grew up together and went to school together. I had been trying to get into medical school. Ben dropped out of college and worked a whole bunch of different jobs, ranging from short-order cook, security guard, taxicab driver in New York City, telephone delivery person, pottery-wheel delivery person, a crafts teacher for emotionally disturbed adolescents, which was his last job before we got together. So he was doing this wide range of things.

We just decided we wanted to do something fun, where we could work for ourselves, be our own bosses, and have a good time. It was going to be a lark. And since we'd both always liked to eat quite a bit, we figured we'd do something with food, and we picked homemade ice cream, and just started with this little ice cream parlor in an abandoned gas station in Burlington, Vermont. We didn't really have any plans to do anything more than that. Through a series of things over many years, the business has grown to where it is now.

But there was never any grand plan. When we got into making ice cream, we thought, "Well, we'll do this for three or four years and then we'll do something else, like become cross-country truck drivers together." We were going to do things that were going to be fun.

Q: Well, it must be a lot more fun to make ice cream than to work for IBM.
Jerry: Definitely.

Q: So how was turning forty for you? A lot of people take that occasion to step back and look at how far they have come in life, and where they are now. Are you where you want to be? Are you happy?
Jerry: Well, you started out asking, would I ever have guessed this was going to happen, and the answer was no. Am I happy? I've done so much more, and experienced so many more things, and tried so many new things that I never would have guessed I would have tried, that I'm really happy about the experiences I've had. There are some things that are still difficult: It's hard to find time to do the things you want to do, it's hard to find a balance among all the important things, whether it's your family, or your job, or your friends, or doing community work, or whatever it is. I think finding a balance continues to be the biggest challenge.

Q: You mentioned community work. A lot of the people who grew up with us in the sixties have lost that sense of idealism—Jerry Rubin is perhaps the prime example.
Jerry: I would not use him as an example for anything. He's the exception that proves the rule.

Q: Well, you and Ben have kept that sense of social responsibility, of course. But so many of the so-called heroes of the counterculture have done a complete turn-around, a hundred and eighty degrees.
Jerry: I think what's unusual about us is not that we've kept our ideals, but that we've been able to integrate those ideals into our normal work life, and integrate them into

the mission of the company. I think for a lot of other people, it tends to be something you do on the side, it's not central to what your normal day-to-day life is, so then you have to find time to fit it in with all the other things you do in life. Whereas if you're able to somehow integrate it, and not separate it, then it's easier to maintain your ideals.

Q: And it's easier to do when you have your own company.

Jerry: Yes. That's not to say that what we do is easy. I think in a lot of ways our company is blazing its own path. We run into a lot of resistance because we're doing things differently, and anytime you try to do something different, you run into resistance.

Q: Did you mind turning forty? Was it a problem?

Jerry: No. You know, it affected me more than I thought it was going to, though, because all my previous birthdays—thirty, thirty-five, whatever—I didn't even blink. I figured forty would be the same, but it was the one where I definitely stopped and thought about it.

Ben and I pretty much turned forty together, our birthdays are four days apart—mine is March 14 and Ben's is March 18—and we have another really close friend whose birthday is March 17. So we planned a "Turning Forty" trip this year. We were going to go on a bicycle trip. We decided we were going to do something that was physically rejuvenating, challenging, and outdoorsy, and so we decided to go on a bike trip. We got permission to get free time from our families. And the day before we were going to go, Fred, this friend of ours, hurt his leg playing soccer, of all things. The ironic thing is that he's the most active and physically fit of all of us.

So instead, we ended up taking a trip to Miami Beach and hanging out on the beach. We got to spend time together, and didn't have to go through the rigors of a physical vacation.

Q: Did you have a birthday party at the company?
Jerry: We had a small party. Generally, we don't, but we actually tried to institute a holiday here several years ago—Founder's Day, to celebrate the birthdays of Ben and Jerry—and the way we'd celebrate it would be to give everyone a day off. We thought, what better way to celebrate? But our people decided they'd rather have time off on Town Meeting Day.

Q: What kind of ice cream did you serve at the party?
Jerry: Boy, I can't even remember. We had a great ice cream cake, it was a beautiful cake. Generally we have multiple flavors of ice cream in an ice cream cake.

Q: What's your favorite?
Jerry: Well, I was really stuck on Heath Bar Crunch for many, many years. Then we came out with Chocolate Fudge Brownie and, more recently, Chocolate Chip Cookie Dough. Now, I'm kind of going back and forth between them. We're just test-marketing frozen yogurt, and I'm heavily into that. It's lighter.

Q: That reminds me, I wanted to ask you what you would recommend for forty-year-olds. Is the low-fat frozen yogurt good for them?
Jerry: Definitely. As Ben says, it has one-eighth the butterfat of our original ice cream, so you can eat eight scoops of frozen yogurt in place of the one scoop of ice cream. That's the way Ben tends to look at things. Obviously you can't eat eight scoops, but . . .

Q: Do you plan any major changes in your life now, having gone through the first forty years?

Jerry: No. I think I'm definitely slowing down physically. I can't stay up all night and work the next day. And I can't eat the way I used to. I can't eat as *much* as I used to. I mean, I just can't fit as much in. Ben and I often lament about it. We can't fit as much into our stomachs. Do you find that's true?

Q: Absolutely, especially at one sitting. And I can't eat as much heavy food, or sweet stuff, but the one dessert I can still have is ice cream.

Jerry: Right. So I think I'm eating slightly differently. I'm more active, I'm more conscious about getting exercise, though I don't do as much violent exercise. I used to play basketball a lot, but I can't take the pounding. So I do a lot more hiking now.

But I do plan on being as adventurous, and doing silly things. I think there's a real tendency, as you get older, to not be silly, and to try to act mature. Ben and I are really lucky in that we can get away with doing just about anything. And we've had each other as friends for so many years that we understand each other, and we can hang out together and do incredibly silly things together, and it's really fun.

Q: What have you learned over the past forty years? What wisdom do you have to offer, after forty years of life?

Jerry: I've learned that there are really no rules about the way things are. Growing up, I always thought that there was a certain way that things should be, or were supposed to be, and I've found out that that's not really true. You don't have to conform to what is considered normal, or what authorities say is right, that it's all bogus.

I think Ben and I are also much more aware of the spiritual dimensions of life, and the interconnectedness of all things. Ben often talks about how everybody's individual welfare is really dependent upon the welfare of others.

STILL MORE FAMOUS PEOPLE WHO, IF YOU ARE 40 YOU HAVE ALREADY LIVED LONGER THAN:

"When Mozart was my age, he had already been dead for two years."   —TOM LEHRER

Died at age:

Buddy Holly	23	Emily Brontë	29
Bonnie Parker	23	Joan of Arc	29
James Dean	24	Anne Boleyn	29
Charlotte Corday	25	Percy Bysshe Shelley	30
Clyde Barrow	25	Nero	31
John Keats	26	Franz Schubert	31
Janis Joplin	27	Akhnaton (Pharaoh	
Crazy Horse	28	of Egypt)	32
Hank Williams	29	Alexander the Great	33
Caligula	29	Eva Braun	33
Jesus	29(–33?)	Jesse James	34

Died at age: (cont.)

Wolfgang Amadeus Mozart	35	George Gershwin	38
Jack "Legs" Diamond	35	Marie Antoinette	38
Henry V of England	35	Stephen Foster	38
Maximilien Robespierre	36	Cleopatra	39
George Gordon, Lord Byron	36	Charlotte Brontë	39
Marilyn Monroe	36	Thomas "Stonewall" Jackson	39
George Armstrong Custer	36	Joseph Smith (Mormon leader)	39
Lou Gehrig	37	Frederic Chopin	39
Mario Lanza	38	Lucrezia Borgia	39
		Martin Luther King	39
		Dylan Thomas	39

LIFE BEGINS AT 40

—PERHAPS

The phrase "Life begins at forty" first entered the American public consciousness in 1932, when a Columbia University journalism professor named Walter B. Pitkin published a thin volume under that very title. Pitkin's thesis was that the circle of Americans who were turning 40 in the 1930s were "the luckiest generation ever":

> Every day brings forth some new thing that adds to the joy of life after forty. Work becomes easy and brief. Play grows richer and longer. Leisure lengthens. Life's afternoon is brighter, warmer, fuller of song; and long before the shadows stretch, every fruit grows ripe.

Acknowledging that physical energy inevitably flags after 40, Pitkin urged his readers to lead "the Simplified Life"—not to be confused with "the Simple Life, which seems to be a career of spinach and raw carrots, five miles from the nearest motion-picture theatre":

As everybody past forty knows well, the job of growing up is largely a matter of sloughing the little desires in favor of the great. We simplify, we pull in, we concentrate on a few powerful, enduring wishes.

Indeed. *Life Begins at Forty* became an immediate best-seller, though one cynic sniffed that its popularity was hardly unexpected: "A book entitled 'Drowning Can Be Fun' would have the same appeal, or one entitled 'There's Money in Being Poor.' " Popular magazines were flooded with articles imitating or rebutting Pitkin's arguments, including "What Begins at Forty?" "Life Ends at Forty," and, most perversely, "Death Begins at Forty."

Undaunted by such mean-spirited caviling, we offer the following reflections on this matter. And if you need further encouragement, you will find at the end of this chapter a list of a few famous individuals who achieved success and/or notoriety only after passing their 40th birthday.

♦ ♦ ♦ ♦

"If I'm not really famous by the time I'm forty, I'm going to kill myself."   —ANDY WARHOL

"At forty a man reaches the top of the hill of life and starts down on the sunset side. The ordinary man, the average man, has at that age succeeded or failed; in either case he has lived all of his life that is likely to be worth recording."   —JOHN HAY

"Is it forty and finished?"   —WINSTON CHURCHILL

"If a man has reached forty or fifty without being heard of, he, indeed, is incapable of commanding respect!"
                        —CONFUCIUS

Reprinted with permission from Hallmark Cards, Inc.

"The real discoveries—the way up the professional ladder, the taking stock of myself, the loves and the friendships, the important books, the irreversible choices—all those were played off during the first forty years."
—SIMONE SIGNORET

"At thirty a man suspects himself a fool;
Knows it at forty, and reforms his plan."
—EDWARD YOUNG

"Take the sum of human achievement in action, in science, in art, in literature—subtract the work of the men above forty, and while we should miss great treasures, even priceless treasures, we would practically be where we are today. . . . The effective, moving, vitalizing work of the world is done between the ages of twenty-five and forty."
—SIR WILLIAM OSLER

"There must be a day or two in a man's life when he is the precise age for something important."
—FRANKLIN P. ADAMS

"At forty I attained to an unperturbed mind."
—MENCIUS

"Invest in yourself until you are forty." —HENRY FORD

"I've always roared with laughter when they say life begins at forty. That's the funniest remark ever. The day I was born was when life began for me." —BETTE DAVIS

"I have been forty years a slave and forty years free, and would be here forty years more to have equal rights for all." —SOJOURNER TRUTH

"What matters is doing things that mean something to you. As you get into your forties, you see that if you're not doing what you want to, you'd better start."
—GLORIA VANDERBILT

"A woman, till five-and-thirty, is only looked upon as a raw girl, and can possibly make no noise in the world till about forty. I don't know what your ladyship may think of this matter; but 'tis a considerable comfort to me, to know there is upon earth such a paradise for old women." —LADY MARY WORTLEY MONTAGU

"Look at Katherine Hepburn. Look at Bette Davis. Some of Hollywood's great actresses came into their primes in their middle 40s because you're better at your work if you let it happen and do not fight the passage of time."
—SHIRLEY MACLAINE

"Nuts to growing old. Don't you ever believe that life begins at forty or that it's wonderful to be seventy. I'd give anything to be thirty again." —BETTE DAVIS

"Certainly one knows more at forty than one did at twenty. And contrary to all American mythology, the novel is the rightful province not of the young but of the middle-aged. Neither genius nor talent is enough, as they are in poetry. The novelist must know a very great deal about the world he is living in. Also, like T. S. Eliot's ideal critic, he must be very intelligent, an innate faculty which needs constant exercise. Finally, he must come to terms with the idea of character as it is affected by time passing, and this takes, literally, time to achieve. In the case of Proust, half a life was lived before he was able to change that tea-soaked rusk into a madeleine." —GORE VIDAL

"Almost all enduring success comes to people after they are forty. For seldom does mature judgment arrive before then." —HENRY FORD

"Hay's idea that we had finished our work in life, passed the summit and were westward bound down-hill, with me two years ahead of him and neither of us with anything further to do as benefactors to mankind, was all a mistake. I had written four books then, possibly five. I have been drowning the world in wisdom ever since, volume after volume." —MARK TWAIN

"This is my real purpose in life. To go through all the major cities and see the mosques. My life just started at 40. All the boxing I did was in training for this. I'm not here training for boxing. I'm going over to those countries for donations. When I get there, I'll stop the whole city." —MUHAMMAD ALI,
before embarking on an exhibition tour to benefit charities

"If you're forty years old and you've never had a failure, you've been deprived. Failure is a part of life too, so better late than never." —GLORIA SWANSON

"Not until I was past forty did I earn enough to marry without seeming to marry for money." —GEORGE BERNARD SHAW

"It is absurd to believe that one can conclude a life of battles at the age of forty-five. . . . I was the leader of the revolution and chief of the government at thirty-nine. Not only have I not finished my job, but I often feel that I have not even begun it." —BENITO MUSSOLINI

"I was forty-five three weeks ago, and between forty-five and fifty-five, I take it, is when a man ought to do the work into which he expects to put most of himself." —WOODROW WILSON

Jacob Cohen, a moderately successful comedian, quit show business at the age of 28 to start a paint business in Englewood, New Jersey. At 40, Cohen decided to give comedy another try. "I owed $20,000," he recalled. "I had two kids. I had problems domestically. Everyone thought I was nuts." During one of his first gigs, the owner of a club decided that Cohen, who had meanwhile changed his name to Jack Roy, needed a better stage name, so Cohen/Roy became Rodney Dangerfield. Less than a year later, Dangerfield appeared on the "Ed Sullivan Show," and his new career took off.

On her 40th birthday, a British Hospital Service employee named P. D. James "realized that there was never going to be a convenient time, that another year had gone by, and still I was not a writer." So Ms. James began rising two hours earlier each morning, spent the extra time writing, and soon finished her first detective novel, which was published in 1962.

◆ ◆ ◆ ◆

Famous After 40

Lucille Ball—At 40, a second-rate film actress stuck in B movies. Two years later, "I Love Lucy" made its television debut.

Samuel Goldwyn—Did not even arrive in Hollywood until the age of 40.

Albert Schweitzer—In his 40th summer, "I awoke from some kind of mental daze"; during a river journey, "there flashed upon my mind, unforeseen and unsought, the phrase 'reverence for life.' The iron door had yielded."

Bonnie Raitt—After a musical career marked by drugs, booze, and a lack of commercial success, she won four Grammys at the age of 40. Ironically, her award-winning album, *Nick of Time*, is largely about coping with the advancing years.

Guion Bluford—At 40, the first black astronaut to travel in space.

Coco Chanel—Introduced Chanel No. 5, "the world's most expensive perfume," just a few weeks after her 40th birthday.

Miguel de Cervantes—Employed as commissary officer in the Spanish Royal Navy at 40. *Don Quixote* lay nearly 20 years in the future.

Henry Rousseau—Quit his job as a customs agent to begin a career as a painter at 41.

Richard Strauss—Composed all his great operas while in his 40s.

Niccolo Machiavelli—Fired from a civil service job in Florence at 43 and kicked out of the city; wrote *The Prince* and *The Art of War* while in exile.

Louis Pasteur—Resigned an administrative job at 44 to go back into the lab to discover why fresh food spoiled in the open air.

Raymond Chandler—At 44, fired from his position as office manager of the South Basin Oil Company in California. Had not written any detective novels by that time.

Alfred Kinsey—Was quietly investigating the behavior of wasps when, at 44, he decided to study human sexual habits instead.

Auguste Rodin—Until the age of 45, spent much of his career making cheap terra-cotta statuettes for the popular market.

Ignatius Loyola—At 47, while visiting Rome, underwent the experience of divine illumination that led him to form the Society of Jesus two years later.

Bela Lugosi—A bit player in second-rate Hollywood dramas until he starred in *Dracula* at the age of 48. ("I am Dracula . . . I bid you welcome.")

Leadbelly—Gave his first concert at 49 after being discovered by a folk music fan while serving time in prison (that is, Leadbelly was in jail, not the fan).

FACTS

1. Americans tend to eat more cereal after they turn 40. According to a spokesman for the Kellogg Corporation, consumers seem to view cereal as part of a healthy diet; hence the increased consumption of Raisin Bran, which is high in fiber content. On the other hand, 40-year-olds also eat a lot more Frosted Flakes than they did at 30.

2. Between September 17, 1990, and June 15, 1991, these were the ten favorite television shows (based on a minimum of ten telecasts or more) of viewers 40–49 years old, as compiled by Nielsen Media Research:

1. "Cheers"
2. "60 Minutes"
3. "NFL Monday Night Football"
4. "America's Funniest People"
   "Murphy Brown" (tie)
6. "Designing Women"
7. "America's Funniest Home Videos"

8. "Wings"
9. "Roseanne"
10. "Unsolved Mysteries"

3. A check of all the last names beginning with "A" in the 1932–33 edition of *Who's Who* showed 98 percent of them to be 40 or older.

4. Anne Bancroft had her first child when she was 40 years old. So did Bette Midler, and ballerina Cynthia Gregory.

5. According to *Harper's Bazaar*, a woman's bangs "can be one of your best assets for a younger look. Yet many women 40 and up shy away from them, assuming they're too old to wear them."

6. On Winston Churchill's 40th birthday, Margot Asquith, the wife of British Prime Minister Herbert Asquith, wrote the following entry in her diary: "Winston Churchill was 40 today. I wrote and congratulated him on his youth. He has done a great deal for a man of 40. When I look round and see as I do a few young men of 35 with amazing brains and see how much less they have done knowing that superiority of character pure and simple is not exactly what Winston has got 'I put myself this question' . . . What is it that gives Winston his preeminence? It certainly is not his mind. I said long ago and with truth that Winston has a noisy mind. Certainly not his judgment—he is constantly very wrong indeed . . . and roughly speaking he is always wrong in his judgment about people. It is of course his courage and color—his amazing mixture of industry and enterprise. He can and does always—all ways put himself in the pool."

7. The American Medical Association recommends checkups at one-to-three-year intervals for people over 40, depending on your present health status, medical history, occupation, and so forth.

8. According to the *New York Times*, the Fields Medal, the highest honor awarded in the field of mathematics, is traditionally given to people under 40, "on the assumption that they will be too old to make further discoveries after that age."

9. Snack foods for consumers over 40 are usually packaged in a box, rather than in a bag, on the assumption that over-40s tend to nibble chips or pretzels rather than gulp a whole package in one sitting.

10. A deceitful person is often referred to as "a 40-faced liar."

11. In the year 2020, the median age of the U.S. population will be 40.

12. In 1971, Pan Am Airlines ran an advertisement which tried to persuade consumers that "the best reason for going to Europe this summer is because you're not getting any younger. . . . Especially when you're 35 or 40 or 50. Because that's the time when we come to understand what getting older really means." Thanks, guys.

13. Bandleader Jimmy Dorsey, born on February 29, 1904, turned 40 on his tenth birthday.

14. In World War II, the British government started drafting 40-year-old men in March 1941.

15. In World War I, there were 688,918 40-year-old men registered for the draft in the United States.

16. Market research reveals that the favorite radio stations among 40-year-olds are those that play classic rock oldies and easy listening music.

17. Billy Carter turned 40 in 1977. I don't know what he was doing at the time, and I don't care.

18. F. Scott Fitzgerald once said that "There are no second acts in American lives," and as far as he was concerned, he was absolutely right. After 40, Fitzgerald wrote only portions of undistinguished screenplays and left behind, at his death, the unfinished manuscript of *The Last Tycoon*. When a reporter visited him in his room around the time of his 40th birthday, Fitzgerald mourned his loss of nerve. "A writer like me must have an utter faith in his star," he said. "I once had it. But through a series of blows, many of them my own fault, something happened to that sense of immunity and I lost my grip."

19. In 1934, the Phoenix Mutual Life Insurance Company ran an advertisement promising to tell customers "how a man of 40 can retire 15 years from today." Apparently it's still a secret.

20. When he was 48, George Santayana walked into his classroom at Harvard, told his students, "It is spring," walked out, and never came back.

21. Ted Williams hit a home run in his last at bat, at the age of 42.

22. Alice Roosevelt Longworth got pregnant for the first and only time when she was 42. "I'm willing to try anything once," she explained.

23. In the comic strip "Peanuts," Charlie Brown once confided to Lucy that his father was going through a rough time: "Every night he sits in the kitchen eating cold cereal and looking at the pictures in his old high school year book." "How old is your father?" asked Lucy. "I think he just turned forty," answered Charlie Brown. "Nothing to worry about," nodded Lucy. "He's right on schedule!"

24. Singer-songwriter Kris Kristofferson, who previously had been (in his own words) "God's own drunk," reportedly stopped drinking altogether at the age of 40. He continued to smoke dope occasionally, however.

25. When actress Meryl Streep turned 40 recently, one of her associates confided that the actress "has gone from being legendary to difficult."

26. A 40-year-old nonsmoking professional person should expect to pay an annual premium of $1,401 for a disability insurance policy with a monthly benefit of $2,500.

27. After the age of 45, German philosopher Friedrich Nietzsche went permanently insane.

28. Syndicated columnist Robert Peterson formerly awarded an annual "Life Begins at Forty" award. Among the first winners were Robert Frost, Harry Truman, Dr. Paul Dudley White, and, at the age of 70, Jack Benny.

29. There is an old Spanish proverb which warns, "From forty years onward, don't get your belly wet." You will just have to use your imagination on that one.

30. In the Old Testament book of Genesis, Isaac was 40 years old when he married Rebekah.

31. Traditional Islamic societies require that men shave and cut their beards no less frequently than every 40 days.

32. There are 40 days in Lent, excluding Sundays.

33. In order to belong to the Forty-Plus club, an organization devoted to finding jobs for out-of-work professionals over 40, prospective members must have earned at least $30,000 per year in an executive position and must have passed their 40th birthday.

34. In Japan, men and women over 40 prefer to refer to themselves not as middle-aged, but as *hataraki-zakari*, in "the full bloom of one's working ability." According to Japanese culture, however, the 42nd year of life is a "danger year," when one should live unobtrusively, buy amulets for protection, and visit shrines to find peace of mind.

35. Psychologist Carl Jung believed that most people make a sharp turn in direction after the age of forty. Instead of trying to use the world for their own purposes, as they had done for the first forty years of their lives, they seek to learn more about the world, about mankind in general, and about their own souls.

36. According to a well-known musical instrument company in New England, an increasing number of men are coping with their midlife crisis by learning to play the saxophone.

37. In Jacobean England, women over forty firmed their breasts with unguent of mint. Middle-aged American colonists preferred the juice of green pineapples as an anti-wrinkle cream.

38. At the age of forty-two, professional wrestler Ed

"Strangler" Lewis, though fat and bald, averaged 150 bouts per year.

39. There are twice as many 39-year-old job applicants as any other age.

40. At 40, you're already too old to be accepted in the CIA training program.